I Found Love

Steve Salmon

CKBooks Publishing

No parts of this book may be reproduced or used in any form without permission from the author except for brief quotations used for articles, posts or in review.

You can contact the author at stevenbsalmon.com

ISBN: 978-1-949085-36-5

Cover art by Majivecka via shutterstock

CKBooks Publishing
PO Box 214
New Glarus, WI 53574
ckbookspublishing.com

watching the Badgers. After forty-seven years, I lived with my Mom and she passed away after a brief illness. Even though my mother died two years ago her loss still hurts.

A month after my mother died, I visited the strip joint to see nude women. My Mom didn't let me go out at night, protecting me from harm.

The Silver Spoon had a bad reputation with fights, drunks, and prostitution, but I felt safe here. A belief among some the strip club was unsafe for a man in a wheelchair.

When I come here, I am rebelling against my mother's memory, against my care attendants, against society. I'm an adult and finally in my life, I'm making decisions that suit me.

It is my day celebrating my birthday at The Silver Spoon enjoying a night out having a beer. I'm escaping loneliness of my group home. No one said, "Happy Birthday, Steve," and there was no birthday cake or a present. It is just another day at my home, but at The Silver Spoon I'm with friends. For the next four hours I'm forgetting my problems and responsibilities, relaxing my mind from the never-ending demands. I can put everything aside for the evening, talking football with Al.

"The Giants killed the Packers. The defense sucks. Are you ready for more beer?" Al picks up the half-filled cup.

"Yes, they should have ran the ball more in the fourth quarter." The Packers lost in the last five seconds of a wild card game when Eli Manning hit O'Dell Beckman for a forty-yard touchdown pass.

I hate to lose at anything. When the Packers lose a play-off game, it is especially painful taking me a while to get over the loss. I have already counted the days until the Packers' first preseason game. The pain of the Packers' loss fades away as I chug more beer.

"You drank half of it," Al holds the beer. I laugh. He sets my Miller down in front of me at the bar.

The Badgers are up by five points at halftime. I strain to see the TV behind Al's head at the bar. TVs are an afterthought in the night club. The TV needs to be bigger and Al needs more TVs, but this is a nightclub, not a sports bar.

Loud sad songs soft rock like "It's A New Life" plays as flashing strobe lights revolve while a stripper dances on the pole. Patrons drink, talking among themselves. Al tells a dirty joke. I can barely hear as the commentator runs through the Big Ten scores during the halftime show. The lights on the stage come on. I soak it all in.

Teenage boys during my generation snuck Playboy or Penthouse magazines into their bedrooms and jacked off leering at the centerfolds. I curse my fisted hand. My disability denied me this rite of passage. With the advent of the Internet, online porn would have made it accessible to me but my mother restricted my access.

It's my new life. I lived with my mother until her death. I'm catching up. Someone taps my shoulder.

"Happy Birthday Steve. Congratulations. Your book is out today," a beautiful brunette says with a smile.

"Thank you, Candy." I inhale her sweet honeysuckle perfume. "It's a big night. I want a dance with you, Star, and Fire."

She rips open the envelope taped to my knee. "Sixty-three dollars; you are celebrating!" Candy hands three bucks to Al for the beer.

A tall redhead, wearing a pink negligee and high heels comes up to me and says, "Happy birthday, my author. Alice gave me your note that you left me a week ago. And I understand what you are feeling." Fire touches my arm.

In the letter I asked Fire to come to work on January 12th. I want to spend part of my birthday with her, celebrating the momentous occasion. The happiness I feel I'm with her is immeasurable. My note to Fire reminds her my books are being released on my birthday and the loss of Mom still hurts. It is bittersweet. I need some love and I know Fire understands what this night means to me.

The emotional moment reminds me how far I have come. I have a book release today on my birthday. I'm lonely. There are times when I feel all alone. I'm on top of the world when Candy holds my hand, "We know. It's a big day and it's hard."

My eyes start to well up with tears, but Fire says, "There's no crying on one's birthday and a book launch."

She shows the cash to Fire. "He wants a dance with Star, you, and me."

"Fuck Star. Just you and me." Fire tells Candy. "Is

that okay with the author?" When she says "Author," I feel as if she is caressing me.

I follow them to a private booth. I feel like a king as my favorite strippers move chairs and tables, making a path wide enough for me in my wheelchair.

Fire pays the bouncer and removes the recliner from the booth. "You go first Candy," Fire says. "I'll have Rob play our song."

After I make a circle, I drive the electric wheelchair into the booth as Candy holds open the swinging doors. She closes the doors and I back up the chair a bit before turning off the wheelchair with my chin, hitting the power button to "off."

Candy waits for a new song to begin dancing. "Just relax and enjoy," Candy seductive voice fills my ears. I nod. When the music starts, she does a strip tease with her negligee. She rubs her buttocks on my boney knee during the entire song. She flips her hair.

My contracted hamstrings prevent a woman from sitting in my lap. I can only imagine putting my member inside of a woman. I watch her breasts and body jiggle making me forget everything. Problems, demands, and emails to write or answer fly out of my mind. My staff are not allowed to call women for me for sex. They will be fired if they do. The world disappears. When the song ends, Candy says, "Happy Birthday."

I don't have time to relish the memory of her touch before Fire comes in and says, "Birthday man, let's make you happy." Our song, "Hey, Big Spender! Hey,

Big Spender! Why Don't You Spend A Little Time with Me," blasts through our room. It's means a lot to me. An author is a distinguished man, spending a little time with a beautiful woman. Fire looks into my eyes, making me melt. She is naked, but the way she stares into my eyes makes me feel like I'm making love to her.

"Fire, would you hold me in your arms?"

"It's your night," Fire says, embracing me while she purrs in my ear.

I don't want the song to end, but reality hits. We stare at each other for a moment, wanting more, but rules prevent her. "Thank you."

I back out of the booth, dreaming of our date and making love with her. I find my voice and say, "Thank you Fire."

› CLOVE HOUSE ‹

The stars twinkle in the night sky as the wheelchair lift lowers. "Good night player," the bus driver says, smiling at me. I roll off the ramp. I smile as I drive to the garage, making a wish on a distant star. My thoughts are on the lap dance and my wish to have a girlfriend. And, of course to have sex.

Lost in my reverie I smack into a snow bank along the driveway. I reverse and straighten my course. The overhead garage door rumbles open. "You shouldn't go to The Silver Spoon. It's a hole in the wall. You're wasting your money. I don't know how you get to go there." Arturo stands in the doorway.

I cross the big bump, entering the garage. The jolt makes me realize that my beautiful evening is over. "I do what I want," I tell him. "It's my life and I had fun."

I roll up the plywood ramp, not answering his stupid question. I cross the threshold, entering into the kitchen. After stopping the electric wheelchair, I say in a demanding voice, "Go pee now." I can't wait to urinate any longer. Even though the staff at The Silver Spoon helps me drink but they can't assist me with the bathroom. My attendants are not allowed to go to a bar with me or serve alcohol to me. It's against the State's rules.

Arturo snickers, "Where did you go?"

"Out." Exerting my independence even though I rely on my attendants for my daily needs. "Pee now." Beer filled my bladder to capacity.

He shakes his head before disappearing in the hallway.

"You are rude and drunk. And you need to come home earlier," says Tawania. She's seated on a black leather sofa in the living room.

"You work for me. I pay you."

"You're being disrespectful again," says Tawania.

Arturo has the urinal and with gloved hands he unzips my fly. Once he pulls opens my Depends, he places my penis inside of the urinal. I take a whiz. Relief.

I'm thirsty. "Water."

Arturo puts me back together.

"Water."

Tawania gets me a cup of water. "You shouldn't be wasting your money at the strip club."

"That's none of your business. I have needs and women make me happy," I say.

The memories play across my face as I smile.

Tawania puts the straw in my mouth and I gulp the water down within seconds. I burp and say, "Take off my coat."

Arturo is back. "You don't tell us what to do." He struggles to take off my tight parka. My body rocks back and forth as he removes the coat. I'm sweaty from wearing my coat for five hours. I don't care. I spent my birthday night with my ladies and Fire. I still want more, including a happy ending. My heart aches for a companion to share the rest of my life with. Thoughts of sex consume me. Dreams are meant to come true, right?

My black cat, Lindy, flicks her long tail at me when she saunters by. "Hi, Lindy. How are you." She waves her tail at me. "I want my manual wheelchair, please."

Tawania and Arturo ignore me, speaking in their native language to each other.

I wonder what they are talking about. Sometimes I speak gibberish to pretend that I'm an African. Often, I ask my care attendants to teach me their native language and what Africa is like. My question is always why they came to frigid Wisconsin.

"Let's go," I say.

My roommate, Jimmy yells, "I have to pee, pee, pee." Over time I have learned tidbits about him. He was married and had two sons. A son drowned in a lake when he was nine. He worked several jobs as a janitor in a hospital and a hotel.

One day he fell and became physically disabled. For several years he lived in a nursing home until he became a resident of Integration Residential Services.

Jimmy gets up about eight in the morning. He takes nineteen different medications with his eggs and bacon or pancakes. Then he watches TV in the living room, but he falls asleep several minutes later. Jimmy is put to bed when his butt starts hurting. For lunch Jimmy eats a ham sandwich with potato chips or a bowl of tomato soup. Late afternoon he might get up to watch reruns of *Roseanne* before having a pot pie or spaghetti for dinner. If he is not in pain, Jimmy stays up for a half of an hour. Usually Jimmy lies in bed, sleeping off and on throughout the day.

On Mondays and Thursdays, he sometimes might go to Catholic Charities from ten to two. When Jimmy arrives home, he is ready to be transferred to bed.

Arturo retrieves my manual wheelchair from my bedroom. He pushes the manual wheelchair close to the electric wheelchair. After he locks the brakes of the manual wheelchair, Arturo goes behind the electric wheelchair and grabs me under my arms. He waits for Tawania to take a hold of my legs after she unbuckles my seat belt. My body stretches in the air. It is a relief to get off my butt for a second. My rear end lands in the manual wheelchair. "Don't kill the author." Arturo and Tawania position me in the manual wheelchair, turning and twisting me in awkward directions. I feel like I'm a rag doll. Arturo fastens the seat belt and asks. "Are you going to work?"

"It's my birthday. I want to watch TV in the office," I say. I yawn, forgoing the book publicity work piled on my desk.

Arturo pushes me down the hallway to the office.

He parks me next to my recliner and in front of my big screen TV. "I want three two on the TV." It's easier for me to say three two instead of thirty-two.

Arturo turns on the TV. The Portland Trailblazers are playing the Golden State Warriors. "Did you want anything?" Arturo asks. I want another beer but I know not to ask him. A full case of Point beer sits under the table with the TV. Drinking is against the Muslim religion (which my caretakers follow) to touch alcohol.

Arturo closes the door. Green and gold decorate my office with Green Bay Packers memorabilia. My framed college degree, pictures of my book covers, a portrait of me, and my grandmother's clay molding of Mineral Point, Wisconsin hang on the wall. My computer and the printer sit on an oak desk.

I am a quadriplegic and have limited use of my arms and legs. A doctor diagnosed me with cerebral palsy, a muscle disorder, when I was six months old. My mother's death in 2015 forced me to leave my home. In one day, due to her death, I was thrust into the company of strangers. I needed a place to live and cannot live alone due to my disability. Clove house is where I now reside. Its lack of warmth and love disqualifies it from being called a home. It is where I need to live.

The Warriors are up by twenty-eight points over the Blazers. I call, "Tawania, my pill." After several minutes, she brings my root beer and meds. I suck the root beer down in one long swig. Then I let out a loud burp.

Tawania leaves.

Charles Barkley on Inside the NBA is like me. I say what I want on my mind which can rub people the wrong way. I don't care.

I look at the clock on the wall above my computer. One o'clock in the morning is early for me. "Tawania, I want to go to bed."

Tawania passes in the hallway with the Hoyer lift, equipment used to lift my heavy and awkward body. She pushes me to my bedroom. She puts the green sling behind my back and then tugs it underneath my legs. Next, she crisscrosses the black straps and hooks the straps to the black iron bars. Tawania unzips my fly and pulls down my Depends, aiming my penis inside of the urinal as I empty my bladder. She raises me, swings the lift to the bed, and lowers me onto the bed, taking off the straps. She pushes the Hoyer out in the hallway. Tawania takes off my blue jeans, tossing them in a laundry basket. She rips my pull ups. She cleans me with baby wipes and a wet warm washcloth before wrestling my drool-drenched sweat-shirt over my tight arms. Tawania rolls me over on my stomach.

I don't *miss* not being able to do these tasks on my own since I never had the ability.

I have lived my entire life dependent on others. What I resent about Clove House is the way they make me feel, like I'm a burden. My mother never did that.

My back and butt relax, but my mind is in overdrive, full of the lust I just left. I stretch my legs and yawn. "Eight zero, please. Thank you. Good night."

Tawania changes the TV to Game Show Network and walks out of the room, closing the door.

I fall asleep while watching *The Newlywed Game*. When the couples talk about sex, it makes me horny and lonely. My dream woman is out there somewhere, but where and when will I find her? Sleep takes away my heartache, making me forget.

I wake up to an info commercial called One Hundred Percent Men. The TV spokesman says, "Guys take One Hundred Percent Men if you can't get or keep an erection. It will make you longer, stronger, and bigger."

In an instant I have an erection. I listen to testimonials, facts, and banter between the spokesman and the two female co-hosts. "I don't need a pill. I need Fire. Give me pussy," I say, rubbing my penis with my left balled fist. I feel the tingle and I put my fingers at the tip of the foreskin, tickling it. When I'm about to come, I press my cock into the bed. I come. It feels so good, but I still want pussy. I fall asleep.

› Morning ‹

I sleep for an hour and wake up at six in the morning. When one of the a.m. shifts-care attendants arrives for work, he slams the front door. "Hello there, Tawania. How are you?" asks Ajay in a loud voice.

I don't hear Tawania's answer. A minute later the door slams again. My left arm swings up and hangs in the air. The arm gets tighter. I can't relax it. I'm awake. I call out, "Hey, hey, hey."

Ajay knocks and opens the door. "Hello there, author. What do you want?" Ajay asks, speaking in his Indian accent.

I look at his bushy grey eyebrows. "Roll over, please."

He returns with gloves. Ajay takes off the sheet and rolls my lower half first. Then he picks up my upper body, tossing me on my back. Ajay moves me to the middle of the bed. "Cover?"

"Yes."

He puts the sheet on me. "Is that all?"

"Six zero."

Ajay changes the channel to CNN and closes the door behind him.

I try to go back to sleep but I can't. My muscles spasm. Ajay clangs the dishes as he puts them away. Indian music plays in the kitchen.

I listen to Ajay's footsteps down the hallway stopping at my roommate's bedroom. A soft knock and I hear, "Good morning, my friend. How are you?"

Jimmy, my roommate yells, "I have to go pee, pee, pee."

Pictures of his family hang on his bedroom's walls but he doesn't talk about his wife or sons.

Rattling and movement echo from Jimmy's room. Ajay says, "Okay, go pee, pee, pee."

It's quiet for a few minutes until I hear Ajay ask, "Do you want to get up?" I don't hear Jimmy's answer, but Ajay says, "I'll be back."

I turn my head to try to sleep. CNN announces that President Trump sent out another tweet overnight about how his low approval rating is a lie created by the news media. He is busy, making America great again. Trump used ghostwriters in his previous books which makes me laugh and say, "You are not a writer. Leave that to real writers. I'm the author, not you."

Then a booming loud voice shakes Clove house. An accessible three-bedroom house adapted for people with disabilities, Ralph, my other roommate, has his bedroom in the basement. Physically able-bodied, he is cognitively impaired. He goes home every weekend to his parents, who spoil him. A calendar in the kitchen has his daily schedule, marking each day's activities plan by his mother for the entire year. Everything must be on time. When something goes wrong like a cab being late or not coming, he will call Mommy and Daddy to get what he wants. Ralph works part-time at a hotel, doing laundry four days a week for three hours in the morning. He is thirty years old with the mind of an eight-year-old. Ralph always asked the same questions and needs constant praise. Ralph laughs when he is nervous and happy.

"Good morning, Ajay. How are you?"

"Good, Ralph. What do you want to eat?" Ajay asks.

"Eggs and bacon. What did you have for breakfast?" Ralph asks.

"Goat cheese," Ajay answers.

"Was it good?" Ralph asks, laughing

"It was good."

"Where are Jimmy and Steve?"

"They're sleeping," Ajay says.

"Why?" Ralph asks, laughing. His laughter is a nervous habit.

Before Ajay can answer Jimmy calls, "Ralph, come here." Jimmy is a kind man. He is lonely and considers Ralph as a friend. Jimmy's mind isn't all there. Ralph enjoys being babied.

"Coming," Ralph says, walking to Jimmy's room. "Hi, Bud. How are you?

"Pretty good, Ralph. How are you?" Jimmy asks.

I lack control over my muscles; hence my body

doesn't respond to what I what it to do, but I'm all there upstairs. In my brain. I am all there.

My roommates wouldn't understand why I'm angry at them. Their insane conversations provide minimal stimulation. I lie there, trying to sleep.

Ralph leaves Jimmy's bedroom. "See you later, Bud." Ralph lives a simple life of attending special activities like basketball and folding sheets at his job. When he has to make a decision, Ralph doesn't know what to do.

"Have a good day at work," Jimmy says.

"Thank you." Ralph walks back into the kitchen.

"Your breakfast is ready," Ajay tells Ralph. "Be careful. It's hot."

"Thank you, Ajay," Ralph says.

It's quiet for several minutes. I have an erection again and rub my balls with my left balled fist, imagining being straddled by Fire. My mind returns to last night. I massage my cock. It takes me longer to come, but after I ejaculate, I fall asleep for fifteen minutes. Ralph asks the same questions to Paula as he did Ajay.

Paula says, "Have a good day at work, Ralph."

"I will." Ralph says, slamming the front door.

I do my best writing at night when the house is quiet and sleep in the morning. I smell bacon and eggs. The smell makes me queasy. I don't eat breakfast.

I hear Ajay and Paula bickering over the hours.

Ajay says, "The p.m. shift didn't do the laundry or mop again."

"They don't do shit. We do everything: give showers, make breakfast and lunch. The p.m. shift cooks supper and puts Jimmy to bed while Steve is out. Overnight sits on their asses," Paula says, grabbing the mop. Jimmy yells like a child for attention. "Paula, my darling."

I listen to CNN. Trump has tweeted about how *Saturday Night Live* writers shouldn't make fun of him and leave writing to real writers.

I'm a writer with a career. You have writers who write for an hour or two while I spend endless hours writing. I'm a statistic, costing the government thousands of dollars, but I'm making a small difference in the world. I fall asleep.

My dreams are vivid: I'm having sex with Fire. Indian music tickles my brain. I cling to this other world. Now Robin Roberts is interviewing me on *Good Morning America* about my bestseller. Loud talking intrudes on my dream. I wake up.

The time is 10:18. I lay there naked as CNN blares on about how America is falling apart according to President Trump, but he will get America back working again.

I should get up and work. With my office in the next room, I don't have to take the bus, riding all over Madison, picking up or dropping off riders. My favorite quotation to say to my attendants is, "You work here, but I live and work here."

I call, "HEY, HEY, HEY."

"Hold on," Paula yells.

Time ticks away. The minute turns into a half an hour as I yawn and stretch. It is 10:58. It's time for me to start my day. I let out a loud shout, "HEY." It pisses me off when people hired to assist me make me feel as if I'm inconveniencing them when I require help.

Paula knocks on the door and enters the room. "You need to learn how to be patient if you ever want a girl-friend. I was busy working." I am your work I want to argue but I don't. It will cause friction and I already have a headache. I smile, thinking about Fire.

"Are you ready for your shower?" Ajay asks, pushing my old manual wheelchair into my bedroom.

I had a regular shower chair with a pail underneath the seat, but my small butt falls through the hole. My rigid muscles make it hard for me to sit in a shower chair. Medicaid won't pay for another one. I asked the wheelchair vendor to order a new shower chair, using some of the money in my trust fund, but he forgot about it. So, I'm stuck with this one.

I had to fight for a daily shower since the staff is "too busy." Staff rules state showers are given at seven a.m. To keep peace, compromises are sometimes necessary.

I emailed the director of the care agency about the problems with my attendants. I have a voice and I will use it. I should be allowed to live my life the way I want and not according to their schedules. My attendants believe I email Jerry, the agency director, all of the time since they receive angry texts and calls from Jerry like "Steve can have all of the bread that he wants and if he wants to eat a loaf of bread feed it to him. If he vomits, clean it up."

My attendants like to say, "Don't email," to me, but all that I do is email. That's what authors do. I have two publishers and a literary agent. Email is my communication to the outside world. My attendants and roommates have learned that anything can happen to me, like being interviewed on the radio, having newspaper reporters come to Clove house, or editorials written by me appear on the local news.

When I open email from my agent with the subject line "Accepted," I turn into a raving lunatic finally accomplishing the impossible dream, waking up the entire house. Eventually it leads to more newspaper articles and radio interviews. It becomes common at Clove House.

Paula uses baby wipes to clean my rectum since I passed gas throughout the morning, leaving bits of excrement. Then she rolls me over on my back. She grabs my legs as Ajay juggles my upper body in his arms.

Ajay takes a hold of my legs.

My stiff body relaxes when I'm up in the air until my butt hits the seat, but Ajay and Paula lift me back more so that I'm sitting upright.

After shifting my body into a more comfortable position, Ajay straps the Velcro seat belt around my thin waist and pushes me into the bathroom. The wheels of the manual wheelchair bounce over the shower threshold. Ajay maneuvers the chair in the stall. He locks the brakes and then gathers towels from my bedroom closet while Paula strips my bed.

I take a leak in the shower. I'm a man. That's what men do in the shower.

Ajay comes back and turns on the shower. The freezing water splashes on my left foot, making me spasm. After the water is warm, Ajay sprays me with the water.

The cascading water relaxes me.

He hangs the shower head up and shampoos my hair. Ajay lathers a washcloth and soaps my body.

I watch him lather my penis, imagining Fire, washing my member. It makes me hard, thinking about Fire and me showering together. I always have an erection the morning after an evening at the strip club and a dance with her.

Ajay washes my face with the washcloth. I squirm when he gets soap in my eyes. He reaches for the shower head to rinse me off.

I savor every second of the shower. My eyes flip open when Ajay abruptly shuts the water off breaking my calm.

He dries my hair, face, and front before pushing me backwards into the room.

Ajay calls for Paula. He stands there, tapping the back of the wheelchair with his hand.

Paula doesn't come. She is on the phone or cooking lunch for Jimmy and Ralph.

I'm getting cold and yell, "Hey, now."

She appears and says, "You won't get a woman that way. You are so impatient."

They transfer me to my newly made bed with a towel. She dries my rear end with another towel.

Ajay returns the manual wheelchair back to the shower. Then he brings Depends, a pair of blue jeans from my closet and a pair of socks from my drawer. He puts my undergarment, socks, and jeans on me. He selects a shirt from the closet and asks, "Is this okay?"

I don't care what I wear unless the Badgers or the Packers are playing. I don't look at the shirt.

A couple of minutes later, Paula appears.

I want to start my day and eat, but I have to wait for Paula to come to help Ajay. I'm tired of waiting every morning for her, but if I say anything to her about it, she will go into a rant. I decide to be patient and quiet to avoid an argument.

"Let's get this man up," Paula tells Ajay.

They lift and position me in my new manual wheelchair.

Ajay straps the seat belt and pushes me to the sink to brush my teeth. He wraps a towel around my neck.

I spit the toothpaste into the towel since I can't rinse in the sink. Ajay removes the towel and pushes me into the dining room.

Paula is on her cell phone, talking to one of her girlfriends, saying, "He did what. Oh, my God. That's serious, girl. Really?"

"I want to eat," I say.

Jimmy is snoring in his electric wheelchair, watching *Bewitched*.

Ajay returns bringing the packet of medication stamped with my name, the date, the time, the dose, and the kind of medication printed on the outside. He makes my iced tea. He rips open the packet and puts the pills all together in my mouth.

I swallow the medication. He gives me the iced tea immediately to wash the pills down. I guzzle half of the iced tea and burp.

"What do you want to eat?"

"Potato chips, please."

Ajay fills a bowl with the chips. He brings it to the dining room and feeds me while he's seated on a stool.

I eat my potato chips, smelling hamburgers, chicken, or TV dinners, cooking in the kitchen. For lunch, I usually snack instead, eating chips, toast, or a piece of fruit. My roommates eat their main meal at noon. I have supper at six unless I go out. Then I eat at four. After fifteen minutes, I'm finished. "Candy, please."

Ajay retrieves a peppermint from my backpack, on the back of my electric wheelchair in the living room.

For an unknown reason, I need to have a peppermint or a lemon drop right after I eat to keep my food down. Doctors don't have an explanation for this mysterious ailment, but it works. Sometimes my attendants forget to give me candy or think that it is unnecessary. But not giving me candy means they might end up with vomit to clean up.

Once I threw up when Teresa neglected to give me candy after I ate Thanksgiving leftovers. She teased me, which made me laugh. And I threw up again.

Ajay places the peppermint in my mouth and asks, "What do you want to do now? Read or write?"

"I want to write. Paula, please take out steak. I want a salad, potatoes, and steak for supper."

Paula nods, while giving Jimmy his insulin.

Ajay positions the wheelchair at the desk. He attaches the head array to the back of the manual wheelchair. Ajay turns on the computer and the big screen TV to CNN.

After I tap the code for the mouse, I move the mouse to the email icon. I double-click it, opening Outlook Express. I hear the front door slam.

"How was work, Ralph?" Ajay asks.

"It was good," Ralph laughs.

I chuckle, too, since I'm just starting my work day.

I listen to Ralph ask the attendants questions. "What did you do? What did you eat, Jimmy? Where is Steve?"

"In the office," Ajay says.

"Why?"

I don't listen to the answer. I am lost in my work. For the next six hours I sit in my green and gold office, emailing my case manager, the director of my care agency, the wheelchair vendor, and do publicity for my books, emailing the news media, trying to get on the local TV, getting an article or a book review in the Wisconsin State Journal. During the day the door slams and Ralph laughs as he comes and goes to basketball practice, the gym, and the bowling alley.

Jimmy is snoring away after being put to bed at one in the afternoon.

I call, "Hey, hey, hey."

Several minutes later, Ajay waddles into the office, "What do you want?"

"I want water, please," I say, slowly since he doesn't understand me that well.

A couple of minutes later, Ajay reappears with a glass and a straw. He puts the straw in my mouth and I gulp it down.

I go back to work.

The attendants' shift changes are noisy out in the living room with their laughing and talking. Doors open and close making me jump.

Jimmy calls for the attendant by name. He knows who is working. "Hello, my darling. How are you?" Jimmy asks the female attendant.

Unlike Jimmy I don't care who is staffed. When I'm working, answering emails, I call, "Hey, come here."

Teresa, Tawania, or Nedie will often say to me, "You are rude. Do you know that? Jimmy is nice."

"I want steak, a salad, and a baked potato at six, Thank you."

I want supper when I want it and I won't be very happy if my food is not ready for me. I'm getting hungry and working all afternoon I want to eat on time. In the past some of my attendants have forgotten to fix my supper. I will yell, complain and cause an argument to ensue.

I finish writing an email to my agent. Publicity is nonstop emailing newspaper reporters, trying to get a feature article in the paper or a book review. When I get a lead or an article, I have no one to share with it. "I have an article in the paper," I tell the p.m. shift.

"So?" says Tawania.

It hurts, but my attendants are clueless about what an author does. I write and answer emails until I hear the front door slam again.

"Tawania, how are you?" Ralph asks, in a loud voice.

"I'm good. How was basketball practice, Ralph?" Tawania asks.

"It was good. Tawania, I want chicken nuggets and French fries."

"I'll call you when the food is ready." I hear Tawania take out something from the freezer.

It is quiet until Jimmy calls out, "I have to pee."

The commotion distracts me. Jimmy yells like a child as Teresa uses the Hoyer to transfer him. His screech grates on my nerves. I take a breath and refocus on my writing.

Tawania shuffles pots, bangs pans, and clangs dishes and silverware in the kitchen. Then the fire alarm goes off. The loud persistent beeping echoes through the house for several minutes, hurting my ears. Tawania thrusts the windows open, letting the smoke out.

I jump goofing up the code for "L." I want to scream. But I don't since it will create an argument with Teresa and Tawania. I don't want to hear that I'm selfish again or I work for my "self-interest." A confrontation would ruin what has been a productive day: I have a lead from the Wisconsin State Journal, I talked to my agent and my two publishers, and I emailed ten papers with my critique to the speech instructor I work for part-time at the technical college.

I laugh inside when Ralph asks Jimmy, "How was your day?"

"I took a nap," Jimmy says.

"Why?"

I don't hear Jimmy's answer.

All that Jimmy does is sleep and eat. He doesn't have any physical energy to do much. Jimmy has given up on living.

For a minute I close my eyes to grab a wink of sleep. When I wake up, I'm hungry. "Tawania, I want to eat."

"Hold on," Tawania says.

Teresa shakes her index finger at me. "You always want something."

I laugh and say, "I don't care. Go pee."

Teresa pushes me to the bathroom door. She rips the Velcro seat belt and unzips my fly. After she pulls down my Depends, Teresa aims my penis inside the urinal.

My food sits on the dining room table with a mug of iced tea and my muscle relaxation medication. Jimmy is asleep. Andy Griffin is on TV. I stare at Teresa and then laugh.

Teresa gives me my medication and iced tea.

I smile, getting my way, drinking half of my tea. The tea cools my parched throat. I eat in rare silence. Ralph is downstairs in his apartment. The steak is chewy. Each bite is delicious. I detect a few lumps in the buttery mashed potatoes. I savor my meal. The rare peace allows me to ponder my accomplishments as a writer. I eye the loaf of French bread on the counter. "I want bread."

"You'll throw up and I'm not cleaning it," Teresa says.

"Give me bread and ice cream," I demand.

"I said no, but you will email Jerry and say that we didn't give you bread. And we will be in trouble. You always get your way." Teresa stares at me like she always does when she knows I'm right. She grabs a slice of bread for me.

Part of me is angry that I have to battle for a couple slices of bread when a simple request should do. It's true I might throw up a meal, but it is a part of Cerebral Palsy. If I'm sick, excited, or don't have my candy I may vomit. My family has countless stories about me, throwing up an entire holiday meal or vomiting in a car while traveling down the interstate. Sometimes I do over eat like everyone else does, but I have learned how much I can handle.

It used to be that I needed an hour to digest my food before I could do anything other than reading or watching TV. It was rare for me to eat out in public. My mother, my cousin, Larry, my sister, Joy, Aunt Kelly, Aunt Becky, and my aides at school were the only people who fed me. Once I threw up in a McDonald's playground in front of other families. It embarrassed me.

Life is different now. I'm on my own. Sometimes when I grab a bite to eat at a restaurant, I rely on friends, strangers, Fire, and bartenders to feed or give me a drink. My friends and fellow writers feed me at the writing conference when my care attendants don't show up.

I remember being at the writing conference with

my agent, Susan, after a long first day. We headed to the mixer to talk business.

"Would you like a drink?" Susan asked me.

"I want a Miller. Thank you."

"Are you sure that you can have a drink. I don't want to get into trouble."

I laughed since twice a week I go out to drink, "I'm an adult man over twenty-one. Mom is gone. I can handle it."

"Yes, you're the author. I'll get the Miller." Susan patted me on the shoulder.

"The author gets what he wants," I say, with a smirk on my face.

"What kind of ice cream do you want?" Tawania asks.

"Elephant Tracks, please."

Women in my life, including Fire, say they know when I want something. My women say that I am predictable just like every other man. The rich chocolate ice cream with chunks of Reese peanut butter cups melt in my mouth. My favorite ice cream is the perfect way to celebrate. When I finish the ice cream, I drink the rest of my tea.

Teresa wipes my mouth with a towel and brushes off bits of food. She washes the dishes, forgetting to give me candy.

"Candy, candy, candy." I stumble over the word in my desperation.

Teresa and Tawania don't hear me until I yell "CANDY."

I taste acid as my food regurgitates up my throat. I'm afraid that I will throw up, but Teresa goes to the backpack on the back of my electric wheelchair, grabbing a lemon drop.

Teresa puts the candy in my mouth, giving me control over my gagging reflex. "What do you want to do now?"

It is harder for me to speak with the candy in my mouth, but I manage to get the words out. "Watch TV in my office."

She pushes me to the office and parks the wheelchair next to my recliner. "What channel do you want?"

"Two four."

I watch the NBA pregame show, sucking on my candy. It is quiet now. I close my eyes for a few minutes, falling in a deep sleep. When I wake up, my body aches, I need to lay down, "I want to go to bed."

"Hold on. We are putting Jimmy down," Teresa says, as Jimmy drives his electric wheelchair into his bedroom.

I'm tired of being told to "Hold on" by Teresa. I don't complain. I know my staff has a routine and Jimmy is put down first. It feels like Jimmy and Ralph always come first as I watch Teresa and Tawania transfer Jimmy to his hospital bed.

Two women change Jimmy. Tawania drives his electric wheelchair out to the living room to charge it.

Teresa speaks in Gambian to Tawania. Tawania appears in the doorway with a grimace and using sarcastic tone of voice, asking,

"What, Steven?"

"I want to lie down."

Tawania and Teresa place me in bed on my stomach. Teresa turns on the TV to *ESPN*, "What time are you getting up?"

"Eight-thirty."

Teresa leaves at nine. I'm a two-person transfer and if I don't get up, I will be in bed until eleven the next morning. I mentally review my to-do list: write another novel, determine the subject for my next article, or compose a post for my website that will compel people to buy my book.

Teresa closes my door.

I watch the Celtics and the Bulls for a few minutes before falling asleep. A burp wakes me up. Acid reflex burns my throat. I have a bowel movement and sleep again. I'm lucky I sleep for an hour. This is a normal evening. It is usually quiet depending on my care attendants. I wake up again and have another bowel movement. I rest watching the basketball game. I keep an eye on the clock. My attendants sometimes forget what time it is and won't change me. Around 8:36 I call, "Hey."

"We hear you." Teresa says.

I hate those words. I hold my tongue and don't remind her I requested assistance at 8:30. It is not worth it. At 8:46 Tawania opens my door with a scowl. "You're impatient and my shift ends in ten minutes."

"I had a bm." I don't care about the shift change. It is a part of my care. I never wait until the last minute.

Tawania changes my Depends. She calls Teresa in African.

Teresa walks into the room, but Jimmy calls for something. She leaves to tend to his needs. After Teresa returns, the women do a two-person transfer lifting me from the manual wheelchair to my bed. It is faster than using the Hoyer.

After I'm in position, Tawania retrieves the urinal for me to pee.

"I want water, please."

Tawania gets my water, places the manual wheelchair in front of the desk, and mounts the head array on the back of the wheelchair. "Are you good?"

I'm back to being an author, ready to write for the next six hours. I start writing the New York best-seller about the stripper and the author.

I'M IN LOVE
WITH A STRIPPER

I sit at the bar, drinking water, waiting for Fire to come to work. I promised Fire I would not drink until she arrives at the nightclub. Alcohol elides my words into a jumble of sounds, making it more difficult to understand me. After several nights trying to have a conversation with me, Fire had asked, "Wait to drink until I get here. So, we can understand each other."

The Badgers are up by five in Iowa. It is still early in the game. Only the regulars are in the bar, drinking and talking about their jobs across the bar. I have a writing career.

"It's hard to make any money these days. I'm making twelve dollars an hour at Rogan's Shoes. It doesn't pay shit. I need a new job." A middle-aged man says to a man with a bald head.

"I'm making twenty an hour, hauling gravel for the new runway at the airport. The Mason Gravel Company is looking for truck drivers if you're interested." The bald men reply, sipping beer.

"Thank you. I'll look into it."

I'm listening to two men talk. Then I ask Al, the bartender, "When is Fire working tonight?"

Al looks at the clipboard. "She'll be here at eight."

I'm giddy inside to see her. I watch the game to pass the time.

"Sam, let's open up the stage," Al tells the DJ.

"This can't be happening," reverberates through the speakers.

"Let's welcome Cookie on stage" Sam announces.

I think about my next novel and revise the plot line. I rework it in my head, satisfied with a new twist. A Wisconsin State Journal reporter sent me a list of questions to answer in a week for the front page of the paper, another journalist wants my bio, and I have a lead for a radio interview.

Tanner gets the rebounds. Two points for the Badgers." The crowd cheers on the TV.

I'm living the life of an author. I want Fire.

I check the score. The Badgers are up by twelve at halftime. I move to the stage to watch the dancers. I tilt the wheelchair back to recline the seat. For a minute I close my eyes.

Fire's sultry voice penetrates my sleep. "Hi, author. What are you up to?"

The fog lifts from my brain. Fire rips open the envelope taped to my knee. She unfolds the letter. "I'll read it at the bar where the light is better."

I turn the wheelchair with my left cheek, following her. Letters always come with the twenty-three dollars. I patiently wait for her to finish reading.

"Al, a Miller for Steve," Fire says, handing him the three dollars. She laughs, making me happy.

"The author has an article coming out in the Wisconsin State Journal."

"Congratulations." Al serves my beer in a plastic cup with a straw and hands it to her. She places the straw near my lips.

"Thank you, I'm making it," I say, drinking the beer. I'm a man with a beautiful woman at my side. I worry that my arm will swing spilling the beer on her, but Fire has learned how to stay away from my left arm.

The beer is refreshing, but I'm like any man, I enjoy a beer after work.

I drink three ounces and I can't get enough of her, dabbing my chin with a napkin. "There you're all clean, my dear." Fire's laugh gives pleasure to all men. It echoes across the establishment, bringing smiles to everyone. "I go up next, but after we'll have our dance, okay?"

I hit the power the wheelchair and drive it back to the stage.

"I'm right behind you," Fire says, carrying my beer. She gives me another swig before putting it on the table. "I'll be back. I have got to smoke downstairs. I know that it's a nasty habit but, like your Mom, I can't quit.

I watch her walk away. Fire is divorced with a teenage daughter who's a cheerleader and on the honor roll. Fire is also blind in one eye and can't drive at night.

Fire knows about my mother's recent death and that I am now on my own. I have told her that I have an agent with two publishers. I also have manly needs. She has read parts of my books. Fire knows that I have uncontrollable bowel movements and my sexual fantasies. She accepts me and my shortcomings as who I am.

Candy sits on a man's lap in the buff. My fantasy goes hardcore as I imagine making love to any woman. I stare at Candy caressing him, wishing that it was me in her arms. "It's A New Life," the jazz song plays. The urge strong, my arm spasms and flings across the table nearly missing my beer. "I want it. I'm tired of waiting. I want it now."

For a few minutes I close my eyes. I calm my body. I'm exhausted. I sleep when I can. Fire taps my shoulder, making me jump.

"You always jump when I touch you."

I laugh, smiling at her. She makes me feel like a man.

She gives me a swig of beer and says, "I'm up next. Then we'll have our dance.

I take another drink. She walks away in a long blue dress, hips swinging, mingling with men. I'm not jealous since I know that it's her job.

Fire gives my twenty to the bouncer in the back. She walks around, flirting with other customers.

The DJ says "Fire is next." I'm spellbound, my eye planted on her body, moving with each sway of her hips, every shake of her ass.

She winks and smiles as if she's only dancing for me.

Fire even comes over to put her chest in my face. "I'll be back." She returns to the stage. The heat from her breast across my cheek leaves an imprint.

I'm happy when she smiles at me again. "I got you. I got you," I say.

She continues to dance. Her hands touch the ceiling as she walks across the stage. Fire takes off her high heels and does a split in front of two men. She points her right index finger to the men beckoning them to come closer. Fire uses her smile and irresistible charm to get the men. She backflips her body on one of the men's laps.

I imagine her doing that to me with her legs above my head as I watch a couple of dollar bills fall on the stage. I picture us alone together. I want Fire more than I want any woman.

When the music ends, the DJ says, "Give it up for Fire. Next is Sun."

It is time for my private dance with Fire. I struggle to turn on the power button with my chin. After several hits with my chin, the wheelchair is on. The anticipation of being with Fire excites me, making my muscles extra tight. I take a deep breath and relax. Fire gathers the money.

She puts her blue dress back on and walks to the bouncer table. Fire gives the twenty to Rick. He examines the bill with a magnifying glass to make sure it's not counterfeit.

He takes the recliner out of the booth and opens the swinging doors for me.

I maneuver the electric wheelchair through the maze of chairs and tables. I'm careful driving past the loud speaker to avoid knocking it over. I turn the corner and the men get up to let me by. After negotiating around a table, I have a clear path to the booth. I drive straight inside. When I situate myself, I turn off the chair with my chin. Fire closes the double doors and sits down. "I'm waiting for a new song to begin."

Would she go out with me? "I'm in Love A Stripper," plays making us laugh.

"That's your second favorite song," Fire says, stretching out her legs on my wheelchair.

I laugh, nerves jumbled in my throat. She is nude. My eyes are on her.

Fire places her breasts in my face for a minute. "You act innocent to people, but you're naughty."

If only I could take you on a virtual trip in my mind, I could show how naughty I am. I melt staring into her eyes.

She stares back.

I need to calm my body. I imagine that we are making love. It is peaceful and I don't want it to end. I'm so happy, but the song eventually ends.

It feels like I'm stirring from a wet dream.

She dresses as I hit the power switch with my chin.

My chin misses the button several times to put the chair into forward. Aggravated, my arm swings wide. Fire's soothing voice brings me back.

"Take it easy."

I take a deep breath. My muscles loosen a bit allowing me to put the wheelchair in reverse. I back out of the booth while she holds the swinging doors open. I hit the power switch and return to my table.

"I'll come by to give you your Miller."

I nod to her. At the table, I tilt the wheelchair back a little before turning it off. I watch the ladies dance.

Fire stops by to give me my drink.

I smile at her as I guzzle the beer down. I don't know when Fire will come to my table again.

"We'll go out soon," Fire says, making me excited. "Email me." She heads downstairs.

I'm not in a big hurry to go home to the loneliness, but I do have to urinate. I ignore the urge, savoring the rest of the evening. "One day I'll have sex. I can't wait anymore. I want it now. I have Fire. I'll have it," I say out aloud, watching the dancers as the music blares away.

MY
OTHER WOMAN

"What did you do this weekend, Paula?" Ralph asks, his voice echoing throughout the house.

In my office, I bristle at the intrusion. I answer an email from a reporter from the Wisconsin State Journal regarding how many books I published for an article she wrote about my writing career. Five books.

A publisher bilked me and I lost the rights to three, of which are now out of print. How naïve I was to sign the first contract to come along in my zeal to be a published author.

I tap in codes with my head to type a reply.

Next an email from a magazine writer distresses me. I'm still working on his request which requires more in-depth thought. I delay him another day.

I yawn.

Ralph says, "I go to work tomorrow, Paula."

I scoff.

"And I'll be working for the next twenty-four hours.

That's how it is being an author. You work when you need to like a farmer does during the planting or the harvest season."

My eyes close for a few minutes, catching a short nap. A ding wakes me up. An email from Heather Davis makes me smile. I click on it.

I can come now. Do u want me?

I tap my three letters reply in capital letters.

YES.

"Hey, hey, hey," I yell.

Paula enters the office.

"I want to go to bed now. Heather is coming."

"You and women. You're wasting your money." Paula takes the head array off and wheels me into my bedroom.

My attendants are one to judge. They're always short on money, yet they're still ordering take-out or picking up fast food. It makes me laugh, too. I have over one thousand dollars in my checking account. Food for me, cat food, baby wipes, lap dances, beer, and the company of Heather. Sex, my guilty pleasure!

"Ajay," Paula calls, taking off my drool drenched shirt.

Ajay comes to the door.

"He has a visitor coming. Help me get him to bed."

They place my rigid body on the bed.

Ajay removes my shoes and socks. He wrestles my blue jeans off my scrawny legs. Ajay rips off my diaper and wipes my butt. When he is finished, he leaves my room.

"Please take out sixty dollars from the lock box and put it on the clock radio," I tell Paula.

She retrieves the cash from the metal box, placing it near the radio. Paula sprays my bedroom with air freshener.

"Please get me a condom," I say.

Paula tosses it on the bed next to my head. The doorbell rings and Paula sends in Heather.

"How are you?" Heather closes the door. She sits on the bed and massages my chest with her hand.

☙

With my new found freedom after my Mom passed, I want sex. Nearing fifty, I was still a virgin.

☙

"I'm busy. I'm tired. Always another deadline." I enjoy the massage.

"I know that you work hard," Heather says, moving her hand down to my member.

"No."

"What do you want?"

"Pussy."

Heather stands up and slowly undresses, exaggerating the removal of each article of clothing. She starts to get into bed, but I stop her.

"Rubber please."

She opens the wrapper and puts the condom on me. Heather positions herself and guides me into her.

I'm in heaven. All my stresses disappear. For a few minutes I savor the time with her. When I'm in her, I watch her ride me, feeling the warmth of her.

Heather moans and says, "More, Steve." She cums.

My flaccid dick shrinks. She removes the condom, throws it in the wastebasket and wipes my member with a tissue. Heather slips on her clothes. "I have got to use the bathroom."

Sex wipes me out.

After a couple of minutes, Heather returns to sit on my bed. "My ride comes in five minutes." Heather rubs my chest again.

I yawn.

"You're amazing. Writing all of the time. In high school I took creative writing. My English teacher said that my stories were good. Maybe I can write a novel." Heather checks her tablet.

"Writing is hard work." I know that she doesn't have a clue what being an author entails. "I'm composing an interview."

"I don't understand what you said. I wish that I understood you more," Heather says to me while texting. "My ride is here."

She slips the money on top of the radio into her purse. "Thank you. I have bills to pay and life isn't easy with my son in jail. And I was evicted from my apartment yesterday."

After I moved in to Clove house, my service coordinator, Emily, said, "Your care attendants can't call women for sex or get you prepared for it. It's considered pimping and an attendant can be terminated."

I strongly argued to convince my care team to allow it. I wrote persuasive posts for my blog about not having sex. I cc'd my posts to my family, friends, case manager, support broker, and Jerry, the Integration Residential Services director, arguing I should be allowed to have sex. In my arguments I reminded others that I'm an adult now with responsibilities. After I hear about a woman with MS in one of the Integration's group homes smoking pot, I fought for my right to have a hooker. Then I learned some of the residents of Integration had visitors in their rooms. I read articles online, saying, "Sex helps relax tight muscles for the disabled," and I put it in the post. Sex was my ultimate dream.

Jerry was tired of my arguments and several times he said to me, "I can't wait until you get laid."

An entire chapter of my newest book was devoted to fantasies of sexual intercourse. When my close ones read about my strong desire for sex, they decided I needed to experiment.

My reasoning swayed my care team I could handle the emotions of sex and they relaxed the rule. Along with most adult males, I craved intimacy, but growing up I was modest only allowing my Mom and Dad to care for my personal needs. As mom aged, I adjusted to having different people assist me with the toilet, changing, and bathing.

A friend of a friend arranged my first meeting with Heather. Money was exchanged with the acquaintance. My counselor, Brian, warned, "That I could can go to jail and have my picture in the newspaper for paying for sex." I didn't care.

Getting caught scared me since bad publicity could ruin my career. Doing something illegal added to my excitement. I waited forty-nine years to have sex. It was an itch I needed scratch.

What does one wear the first time one meets a hooker? I opted for comfort, sweat pants, sans Depends, and an undershirt. Lying on my bed or sitting in my chair? I had showered and shaved, with a slap of cologne from Ajay for good measure. Was it too much? I smelled myself. Nervous, I willed the clock to move. Time inched forward.

My chest constricted and my body tensed when the doorbell rang. Voices in the hallway came closer. My heart pounded.

To calm myself, I took a deep breath.

Paula brought Heather into my bedroom and closed the door. I sat frozen in my wheelchair.

"I'm Heather." She embraced me for a moment.

I started to cry. My Mom gave me daily hugs and I missed them.

I stumbled over my words and instead chose to be

quiet. Heather and I sat in my bedroom. My member throbbed with her next to me.

She slowly raised her shirt revealing her breasts. The milky white contrasted with her tan lines.

I panted and drool spilled from my mouth.

She stood close to me and slid her jeans down her thighs revealing her triangle. She rubbed her vagina and then my crotch.

Overload!

I came before Heather pulled down my sweat pants. Heather sucked me. She moaned, flicking my foreskin with her tongue. Heather took my member out of her mouth and said, "You are not a virgin anymore."

My body was electrified. High voltage cursed through my body. Sex was wonderful. After she left, I felt empty inside. I had overdosed on the most wonderful drug and coming off the high only exacerbated my isolation.

I would tolerate the lows to have that high again. I wanted more.

Heather serves her purpose. Is she scamming for a bigger tip? I listen to her but I don't care. Other people can keep their problems. I always have issues to figure out by myself. My care attendants harp about their personal trouble daily. I tune them out.

My mind focuses on my problems. It's up to me to solve them.

She covers me with a blanket. On her way out, Heather says, "I love you."

Heather doesn't love me. She loves money.

LIFE AND LONELINESS

"Women. I love women. Women are awesome. I'm a man."

For years I thought I would never have sex, living with Mom. Now I'm on my own and sex is still new to me and full of wonderment. Fantasies of the past can come true. I look at my member and smile. My body is relaxed. I fall into a deep sleep. An hour later, I wake up. I'm hungry, but I want to get some more rest before getting up. I try to go to back to sleep but I can't.

It is seven when I call, "Hey, hey, hey."

"Hold on." Kerry calls back.

"Back to reality." I say to it myself. Time ticks away, but I wait, knowing that I will be up all night.

"I shouldn't be able to hear you two in here," Kerry says, walking past me to get a change of clothes. "I shouldn't allow it since it is against the rules."

Technically by the State's rules residents in group homes are not allowed to have a prostitute visit, but Integration director, Jerry decided to let me. Kerry, the case manager at the Clove house, was teasing me about "It is against the rules," trying to get a rise out of me.

I choose to ignore Kerry's dry wit, knowing I have permission from Jerry to have Heather over.

Kerry manages Clove with authority, but she has to abide by Jerry's decision for a female visitor to see me.

I sit in the office, wearing socks, sweat pants, and an undershirt, waiting for Heather. I'm nervous meeting Heather for the first time. My member is hard in anticipation of sex and I'm trying to not come yet. I wonder what Heather looks like. My mind is racing while I wait.

Maybe I'm not ready for this. Mom wouldn't like it, but I see the bulge in my sweats, getting bigger. Time moves on as I keep waiting for her. Where is she, I ponder? I watch the clock, ticking away making me fear she isn't coming.

Heather might be an undercover policewoman here to arrest me.

Jerry and my counselor, Brian warned me if I get caught, I face the consequences.

Time doesn't stop. There is no sign of Heather. It makes me think she won't be visiting.

I'm disappointed. I start to ease my concerns about the evening. Then I jump when the doorbell rings. My heart and thing are pounding when I hear Kerry answer the door, hearing, "Welcome, he has been waiting for you. I'll go get him."

I start to excited when Kerry comes. When I see

Heather, she hugs me. I begin to fall in love, but in the back of my mind I hear my friend, Charles, saying, "She is a visitor not a girlfriend. Once she is done, she is gone."

I'm enjoying the moment with her, embracing me. I try to remember this isn't love, but it feels like it is.

Sex consumes me. I don't care. With all I have to do myself, I view me as an adult in a wheelchair, making every decision. I know right from wrong.

I can protect myself unlike someone like Ralph, who is sheltered by his parents and the system. The system tends to group people with disabilities together applying the same rules to each disabled person.

Individuals have to follow these safeguards, but in this case, I won the battle, proving to Jerry I'm willing to accept the positives and the negatives of paying Heather for sex.

My muscles are relaxed after intercourse. I'm beginning to tense knowing I have a deadline to meet. "Let's go," I say to Kerry, seeing her pull up my new Depends on my hips.

"Will you hold your horses. I'm getting you up now." Kerry dresses my rigid body in a few minutes. "Teresa, I'm ready to move Steven."

Teresa pops her head in the doorway, wearing gloves. She gives me a disgusted, sarcastic look and sighs.

"Teresa, my dear. Come here," Jimmy says.

"I'm helping Kerry, Jimmy," Teresa says, grabbing my legs while Kerry takes my upper torso.

I'm lifted and positioned in the manual wheelchair by the two women. "Go pee," I say.

Kerry stops at the bathroom to assist me with the urinal. Then she pushes me to my desk in my office.

"Water please." I tap the buddy button, waking up the computer.

"I'll bring it in a while."

Kerry walks out of the office.

I tap out my response for the magazine interview. Four TVs are on throughout the house. Sports Center is on in the office and my cat, Lindy lies on the top of the recliner, keeping me company. Kerry is talking on her cell phone, doing paperwork, and listening to music on her iPad.

I keep my head swaying back and forth as the clock ticks away. I don't notice when Kerry brings my water. I suck down the water in an instant. I'm in a zone.

"Kerry, baby. I dropped my remote." Jimmy calls her.

Usually at this time of night I would be working on my next novel, but I'm spending time, stringing words together writing detailed answers for the interview.

"There you go." Kerry says.

"Thank you, my darling."

The doorbell rings and Kerry answers it. I hear an exchange of greetings but not what is being said. I'm writing efficiently and avoiding mistakes when Tawania comes into the office, surprising me with a glass of water without me asking. "What's up, Steve?"

"I'm busy. I need to finish by tonight. I want water. Thank you." At times some people don't understand my speech. When I'm short, I avoid the niceties.

"You're rude." Tawania walks out of my office.

I try to ignore her comment, focusing on writing the answers, but her reply strung.

Other care attendants have called me an awful person. The words shatter pieces of my heart. I often have negative thoughts during these times. I'm a sensitive person. The words threaten my self-confidence. For a half hour, I mutter to myself, "I'm rude. I'm an asshole. Maybe I ought to kill myself. I'm just a failure."

After I calm down, I build myself back up by listing my positives. I have a writing career and an agent. Friends believe in my talent. I'm making it. Why die now? Come on, Steve. Get going. I have got work to do.

After a deep breath, I sway my head back and forth tapping Morse code methodically. Every five seconds a new character pops up on the computer screen. It is a slow process.

My mother put me through college, being a home-school aide, sacrificing her life in her devotion to me. She moved five times, bought four houses, paid for my education, bought computers, turned countless pages, and cared for me without help. Mom never complained and didn't get a break all those years. Her belief in me is why I'm writing my new manuscript and getting this interview done.

My butt hurts. It's going to be a long night.

Dan Patrick, a sports commentator, talks about writers as sports highlights play on TV.

I hear Dan Patrick making fun of writers and I laugh,

asking to myself, "What do writers know? Writers are dumb people. They think they know everything and that all writers do is writing. Thank God, I'm not a writer." I say, joking with myself.

I'm thinking about getting done concentrating on writing my answers. Time ticks by. I feel like I'm a truck driver, counting the mile markers pass by in the dead of night as I head toward my destination. My eyes start to close, but I fight to stay awake. I nod off for a few minutes but I wake up with renewed energy as I continue to write.

Jimmy's hospital bed creaks whenever he raises or lowers it. At times Jimmy calls for Tawania to urinate or for the remote control. Most of the time he sleeps throughout the night, but he wakes up at 4 a.m. to watch *Doogie Howser* for some reason.

Tawania gives me my medications with root beer.

It's late even for me, but I'm on a roll. One more question to go. Clove house is silent making it easier to write. Why stop now? My back and butt are hurting, but I ignore the pain.

I meet Tom's deadline. I always keep my word. It is 5:22 a.m. I stretch my neck as best I can.

Lindy on the top of the recliner winks her big gold and green eyes at me before going back to sleep. I answer the last question.

What are your dreams for the future?
I want my own apartment where I can sleep in peace, but my biggest wish is to have a girlfriend to

share the rest of my life with. I want a woman to go out to eat with, to talk to, to love, and make love to. We would live together and get married. I don't want to be alone. It hurts. Maybe someday I will find her. Anything is possible like publishing two books in a year as I have done. That's my dream. A man needs a woman to make him think beyond himself and enjoy life.

"Ajay," Jimmy calls.

"Coming." Jimmy's door squeaks as it opens.

I'm exhausted. I save the document and shut down the computer. The document needs a final edit but I can't stay awake. I wait until Ajay is finished with Jimmy.

"Hey, I want to go to bed," I say.

"The author is still up."

"Bed, please."

> Sal's Saloon <

I'm napping at the dining room table after lunch when Ralph says, "He isn't awake, Paula."

"Shut up." I raise my head to look at Ralph.

"Paula, he said shut up to me. That's wrong. Shut up isn't nice." Ralph eats his pizza.

"Shut up," I repeat to irk him, yawning.

"He did it again. Shut up is bad. He is evil."

"Shut up." My goal is to send him over the edge. I'm having trouble keeping my eyes open. "Take me to the office."

Paula pushes me to the office, setting me up at my computer to write.

"Paula, I'll finish these edits and send the interview.

"I'm going out tonight." Going out by myself to the bar, the strip club, or anywhere when I lived with Mom was not possible. Mom controlled everything I did, where I went, when I ate, when I got up, and when I went to bed.

It's my life now and I'm going to the bar to enjoy a night out. "Please call the bus for Sal's tonight. I need a beer."

I proofread the interview, making the final edits. I attach the Word document to the email and send. Next, I compose a message to Jerry, the director of Integration Residents Services to head off flak for yelling at Ralph.

Mark, the bus driver opens the front door of the saloon for me. "Have a good time, player."

I bump into whiskey barrels. I drive past dart boards, pool tables, and pop-a-shots, heading to the bar. The smell of beer draws me in. Banners of the Big Ten schools dangle from the ceiling.

"Hi, Steve," Doug says, moving a couple of stools out of the way.

My cheek taps the power switch. "Hi, Doug." Purdue and Wisconsin play on the big screen TV. Wisconsin trails by five.

"What will it be, Steve?" the bartender asks.

"Miller."

Doug carefully positions the straw. I sip the cool refreshing beer.

My tense muscles relax a bit. Doug sets the glass down on the bar. My electric wheelchair is a foot lower than the bar. "Tell me when you want more." Doug returns to watching the Brewers versus the Angels on his tablet with me sitting next to him.

I check out the UCLA-USC game to the right and the Indiana-Penn State game to the left. When I want to see multiple games at the same time, I come to Sal's.

Fuzzy pats me on my shoulder, saying, "I thought we wouldn't see you until football season. I'm still not over the Packers losing to the Falcons in the championship game."

"I hate to lose. Next year we'll win the Super Bowl." I smile. "More beer, Doug."

Doug gives me sip. "We need a running back and safeties. The secondary sucks."

I enjoy the conversation because I can't talk sports at home. The Badgers are losing by ten at the half.

"We need a guard, too." Fuzzy gives me another sip of beer.

"Thank you."

"No problem."

"The Badgers suck." Fuzzy downs a Coke and rum. "I have work in the morning and I should go. But I'll stay for a while longer."

Work doesn't end for me. I will go home to work until three in the morning. For now, I'm a man relaxing with two friends. "I was up all night, writing an interview for *Our Town Magazine*. The deadline was today," I say with pride.

"What do you do?" Allen asks.

"I'm an author." I see that my two new friends don't understand. It is frustrating. I want them to understand what I do. I try again, "I write books. Two books were published this year."

I return to watching the game.

In the second half of the Badgers game with sixteen

minutes to go, Wisconsin cuts the lead to six. The three of us watch the game and drink. The saloon fills up with college students and music plays. The crowded bar hops with patrons who are buying drinks. Bartenders run back and forth filling orders. The Badgers take the lead at the eleven-minute mark, hitting four three-point baskets in a row.

"Beer please." I look at Doug.

Doug holds the straw for me to drink the four ounces of warm flat Miller.

I drain it.

"See ya later, Steve." Doug puts his empty glass on the bar.

"Yeah later." Fuzzy pats me on my shoulder.

Doug and Fuzzy leave the bar. I watch the rest of the game, listening to the soft rock music as the students jockey for position at the bar.

Loud conversations rumble around me. Patrons bump the readout and the head array on the electric wheelchair, making me nervous that a person might unplug a wire by accident, leaving me stuck there. Music blares through speakers and the DJ announces drink specials. The crowd drinks, sings, and dances.

I soak in the festive atmosphere. I'm relaxed. The song "It's A New Life," and "I Do What I Want," remind me of my new life.

With my terrific eyesight, I can see across the bar the time on one of the cash registers reads 10:09. I slowly make my way to the door. My chin turns the power switch and a second hit puts the wheelchair in reverse. Then I touch the switch again, easing the chair through the crowd. I smile at people who tell their friends to move out of my path. When I get near the door, I park a couple of feet away from the pool tables to avoid getting hit by the pool stick.

Men in yellow shirts card those lined at the door to get in.

I feel a sudden urge to urinate. A bouncer tells me the bus is here.

"Thank you." The bouncer clears a path, asking people to move.

Another half hour until relief.

› HOME ‹

"The p.m. shift didn't do the laundry again. They don't do shit." Paula says.

They continue to bicker while I'm naked in the shower.

"Hey."

"Be patient." Paula tells me.

I'm powerless waiting in the stall as the complaining continues. I lose patience. When Mom was alive, I was the center of her universe. Here I have been relegated to an intergalactic spec floating in the outer fringe, a nuisance when I enter their orbit. "Hey!" The cold makes my muscles extra tight.

Ajay walks into the bathroom.

Later I ask Paula, "Can you call the bus? I want to go to The Silver Spoon tomorrow night to see Fire."

Paula is on her cell phone, talking to a friend. She doesn't answer me until she finishes the call. "Ask the second shift to call. I'm not doing it all anymore."

It annoys me. You can't get blood from a turnip and

you surely can't coordinate dexterity from pelagic limbs. I wait for evening to ask Teresa and Tawania to call for the bus. I also ask her to bring me some French bread.

"That's Paula's job." Tawania sits on the sofa, eating her supper.

Teresa gives me a sarcastic expression. "I have got to cook dinner. Don't email Jerry. That's all you do." Teresa waves her right index finger at me.

"I want to write in my office," I demand, wanting to escape the craziness of Clove house happening with the staff. Sometimes it gets so overwhelming with the attendants becoming hard to handle, the constant backstabbing, and the endless noise makes me want to be alone. It's like dodge ball, I'm slammed by a team of relentless bullies. I have a weapon. My staff expects me to email Jerry when I'm not getting what I want or need.

And I do. He will call Clove house and say, "Give Steve what he wants."

I should be able to make my own decisions. My case manager, Kerry, decided I had to wait to eat ice cream after I get up from my nap when I vomited an entire dinner one evening. Then they decided not give me any ice cream anymore, but ice cream is how I get my calcium.

I don't drink milk. When I emailed Jerry, he sided with me.

I snack at lunch and supper is my main meal of the day. I have done this all of my life.

I have to wait until ten to eat my ice cream when Kerry is working in the house. But when my other care attendants work the p.m. shift, I have ice cream for dessert. It is frustrating at times.

I'm at the mercy of my staff. I can't force them physically to do anything, but I can or have care attendants removed from Clove by numerous emails to Jerry. When an attendant, who was African had trouble understanding me and would ignore what I asked for. I tried to be clear in my speech when I talked to her. After sending several emails to Jerry and Kerry complaining about her, it didn't work. One night she worked overnight and about two a.m. she left Clove to tend to her sick baby. I emailed Jerry and Kerry reporting the incident.

Then I peed in my pants while I kept writing until the morning. At 6:48 the front door slams, a minute later Kerry walks into the office, finding me, sitting at the computer with a big puddle underneath my desk. "She's out of here now. I'll clean you up and put you to bed right now," Kerry says, pushing me into my room while answering a call from Jerry.

"What are you doing?" Tawania walks into my office.

I ignore her. I'm in my writing zone, following up on a lead to a newspaper article. "What do you want?" I continue, tapping away on the computer.

Tawania reads the follow-up from The Capital Times and says, "Everything that you do is for your self-interest."

I'm promoting my book. "I have got to sell my two books and I'm doing PR." I continue to write.

"What is PR?" Tawania watches me work.

"Public relations and I hate it. Now go away, please."

"You're rude." Tawania walks out of the office.

My mind is on nailing down the interview for The Isthmus article. I send the email. An hour later I receive a yes from the reporter. All of this work feels like digging or pulling a stump out of the ground. "The author wins again."

"Tawania, Tawania, I want to eat. Tawania, I'm hungry."

Tawania appears several minutes later with a sullen face. "I'm not talking to you."

It's a game we play. I'm contrite and she performs what she is hired to do. "Okay, I'm sorry. I have got another interview to do. I'm making it." I would pat myself on my back physically if I could.

"So? Who cares? All that you care about is you, writing, and women."

Tawania pushes me into the dining room.

I care about people and the world around me. My staff really doesn't know how caring I can be. Sometimes I want to help them when they need money, but it is against the rules. I do care about my staff even buying a bicycle for one of my attendant's three-old-year daughter's birthday.

I appease her by saying, "I'm awful I guess." I know she's wrong. Her words sting and I consider quitting. I feel sorry for myself. I imagine being at the Memorial Union, driving my electric wheelchair off the pier into Lake Mendota. A giant splash of water, people try to save me, but it's too late. The wheelchair sinks to the bottom of the murky water.

If I never succeed, I have spent my life writing it away. The endless work wondering what am I doing? An attendant can dash my sense of accomplishment with a few negative words.

I have had positive outcomes along the long bumpy road I'm traveling.

No one to share the moment with me. No one to hug me. No one to pat me on my shoulder and say congratulations. The same is true when nothing goes right and rejections fill my inbox. An embrace soothes a broken heart.

I can email my vast network of friends, including authors for encouragement or to celebrate. Email takes time to write, receive a reply, and can't substitute for the human touch. My friends' kind words help me move forward, but I want a partner to say, "Steve, it'll be okay. I love you."

I know many people adore me and admire me. Readers of my books love me, but the negativity from my staff threatens to destroy my mental outlook.

When I'm having a bad day with my staff, I remind myself what thankfully fellow authors have said, "You're living the good life, Steve," or "No one can do what you do." I cling to those affirmations.

MEMORIAL UNION

It's peaceful as I sit on the UW Union Terrace Stage watching the sail boats on Lake Mendota. I close my eyes, relaxing in the shade, enjoying the quiet. No care attendants tell me, "I'm awful," or staff on their cell phones, yakking about their problems.

I imagine driving into the lake. My mind is composing the next chapter of my newest manuscript. The crystal blue water with the cloudless sky creates a picturesque scene, maples and oaks, lining the outer banks. I fall asleep for a while. When I wake up, I look at Lake Mendota.

I could end my life right now if I choose.

Even though I don't have much physical control over my body, I have the mental capacity of deciding what happens with a flick of a switch, making it look like an accident. I see how living is. A cool breeze blows. The scent of brats on the grill engulfs the air. Families and couples enjoy the perfect Sunday afternoon. People sit on picnic tables or the iconic colorful wrought-iron chairs, eating, drinking, and talking.

Dogs with their owners make me think of Lindy, my cat. I cat nap while I develop characters in my head. Women in bikinis sunbathe on the piers. Music floats in the air.

I hear the song, "I Love Your Body." Fire comes to mind. I'm making love to her.

I scan the crowd for couples, hugging, holding hands, and kissing. I know this is what partners do. It hurts me to see two people in love. Will I find someone for me? I wish a woman would walk up to me and see me for who I am and not the body I present. I fear love might not happen.

I fall asleep to escape the pain, a respite from my unfulfilled dreams, demands, and I move the wheelchair down to the pier to look at women in bikinis. Then I leave the stage, traveling a short ride, taking me past Alumni Park and the Red Gym. I park the wheelchair a few feet away from the dirty water. The chair is off and I catnap again. Honking overhead wakes me up. Another duck floats in the dirty algae water, fighting its way to a better place. I look at women, sunbathing in different positions. I think of sex.

The patter of footfalls wakes me. Two small children walk by with chocolate ice cream, dripping down their hands from their waffle cones. Their mother trails them, licking vanilla ice cream from a sugar cone. My stomach rumbles. I want ice cream.

It frustrates me that I won't have ice cream because no one is here to feed me. In order to save money, Jerry has cut weekend hours to only one attendant per shift. Jimmy is asleep in his bed, tying Tawania to Clove house. Hence, an attendant isn't with me right now. I could become like my roommate, Jimmy, and sleep away reality. Jimmy takes a lot of meditations, making him sleepy. He also suffers from depression. Instead I envision a girl-friend—we would share a caramel-sundae with nuts and a red cherry on top, one spoon.

› INDEPENDENCE ‹

Decisions, decisions, decisions. Big, medium, and small decisions that I need to make each day pour down like sheets of rain.

Early Saturday morning I'm on the bus to the farmers' market to buy fresh picked strawberries for my favorite dessert, strawberry shortcake with vanilla ice cream. I would have rather slept in, but the days of my mother grocery shopping while leaving me at home are long gone.

On the crowed sidewalk, I am vigilant that I don't want to run over a toddler. I stop and start every couple of feet. Sometimes I bump into people and often I hit a pretty woman on purpose. I weave in and out of the crowd, until a stand with spinach, beets, snap peas, and green beans catches my eyes. I want everything.

"I want that and that." I stare at the spinach and the snap peas.

The man follows my eyes. "Peas and spinach?" He put the food in the backpack.

"I have got money in the back." I know the man feels sorry for me not trying to look or take my money. It makes me feel like a cripple, but I know my speech is very difficult to understand and my drooling doesn't help matters. I want the vegetables even though I want to pay for them, but I decide to keep moving with the free vegetables. It leaves a guilty feeling with me but I had no choice.

The man returns to his stand without being paid.

I search for strawberries. Grocery store strawberries don't compare to fresh grown.

I roll past Stella's Bakery stand with its different breads and soft pretzels. The aroma of sweet rolls, cookies, and muffins tantalize my taste buds. My saliva glands go into overdrive, but I only have twenty dollars.

"Where are the strawberries? Then I see the strawberries. The vendor has tomatoes, too. "I want that and that," I eye the strawberries first and then tomatoes.

"You want the strawberries and the tomatoes?" The gentleman bags the produce with a questioning expression on his face. "Ten dollars." It's instinctual for him to hold out his left hand out for the money and to hand me the bag with his right.

I smile at him, putting the man at ease. "I have got it in the back." I turn my wheelchair, giving him access to my backpack.

"Where is your money?"

"In the back." I point my head towards the backpack.

The man steps from the stand and goes behind the

wheelchair. A minute later he finds my wallet and shows me when he takes out two five-dollar bills. The man puts the billfold back in the backpack. "You're ready to go."

I meander through the crowd. I feel good about the healthy food I got today and spending just ten dollars. Kerry does the bulk of the grocery shopping for the house.

On Wisconsin Avenue in front of the Concourse Hotel, I wait for the bus.

I attended a writing conference here each April for the last twenty years. I look into the windows of the conference room. This is where writers pitch their manuscripts to literary agents and how I met my agent. People on the street look at me as I talk to myself, "Next year I'm getting a big-time agent and becoming a New York author. I'm going to New York to tell my story on *Good Morning America* to the world. Someday I'll make it." I'm dreaming again.

Pedestrians shy away from me, a person with a cognitive disability, or maybe mentally unstable.

I'm ready for a nap. I tilt the electric wheelchair's seat upwards giving my butt a break. I'm getting old. My body aches at times. I take a cat nap in front of the entrance of the hotel, basking in the sun. I wake up a few minutes later in pain.

My butt hurts from the too firm seat. I emailed the wheelchair vendor, Matt, to order a cushier seat after trying two others. The wheelchair is new; Medicaid and Medicare won't pay for a new three hundred- and fifty-dollars seat. When Matt delivered it, I couldn't privately pay for the seat. My beneficiary agency refuses to pay the same payee any amount over twenty-two hundred in the same year even though I have two thousand dollars in my checking account.

After buying a shower chair for nineteen hundred dollars, the seat brings me over the limit. Shower chairs are not a medical necessity according to Medicaid and Medicare taking a year to approve a shower chair.

The first shower chair with a pail underneath didn't work for me. My butt fell through the toilet hole. I had been using an old manual wheelchair to shower in until Ajay said, "This chair is not good. It's moldy."

After forty-eight years of taking bed baths, I now enjoy showers. I bought a Packer yellow shower chair to avoid hearing Ajay and Paula complain about the mold. I used my trust fund money to bypass the thirteen-month wait.

I call the shots now. Everything is on me. I planned my own funeral with the help of a funeral home director just five months after mother's death. My decision is to be cremated. I chose my urn, wrote my obituary, named my agents of my last rites, picked out songs, planned the menu, and paid for the memorial service. My tombstone will say: "Steven Salmon author Packer fan." My trust fund paid for the eight-thousand-dollar funeral. It costs a lot of money to die.

Death pops into my mind when Teresa says, "All that you care about is you." Or when Tawania tells me, "You're selfish for not sharing your pizza with Jimmy."

I'm watching a Packers game, cheering on my team, when Teresa says, "You're disturbing Jimmy."

"I don't care. All he does is sleep" I'm yelling. "It's game day. I'm in my office and I'm going to enjoy my day off. His missing some three hours sleep won't hurt him."

"Football is on all day. Packers are playing the Vikings. It is a division game. It is war."

"Jimmy needs his sleep. You're rude." Tawania slams the office door shut.

"Hey, hey, hey. How dare you? You can't shut the door. Come back here now. Jimmy sleeps all of the time. He doesn't do anything. I work all week and it's game day. He is just a vegetable. Hey, hey, hey." I lash out in anger.

It doesn't seem like my staff care about me or my interests. Loneliness cloaks my spirit. I dwell on the concept of death—I could die almost happy. I have accomplished what I wanted except having a girlfriend.

Tawania opens the door, pointing her left index finger at me. "You're rude. What do you want?"

"Water and make chicken for supper, please. Thank you."

Aaron Rodgers throws a pass at the five-yard line.

Tawania blocks the TV with her body. The crowd roars on TV. "All that you care about is football, writing, and women. Jimmy is nice and you're mean."

"Get out of the way." I missed the touchdown pass. "Packers, Packers, Packers. Like the author!"

When the Packers win or Aaron Rodgers throws a touchdown I yell, "Like the author." Because an author wins or loses. A touchdown reminds me of the hard work of getting published, being interviewed, or writing a news editorial.

› WOMEN ‹

My hands sweat as I struggle to compose a letter to Fire. She was the first stripper who took the time to sit and talk to me. Maybe she approached me because she was curious about the man in the wheelchair. Patient, she deciphered my slurred speech to learn about me. I'm ready to take it to the next level. The first step to a deeper relationship is requesting a date.

I ask her to join me for dinner when I attend the writers' conference at the Madison Concourse Hotel. I plan to spend the weekend and invite her to my room afterwards to spend time alone. With my anticipated success of our first date, my mind spins an end to our long romantic affair. An author creates his story:

"Who are those women?" I picture my sister, Joy, at my funeral asking my three female college classmates, who the red head clad in a mini skirt and crop top, bangles on her arms, wearing five-inch spikes and why is Fire here.

"I'm afraid to ask," Mary, one of my classmates would say.

"When his mother died, Steve, couldn't go without women for very long," Patti would respond, smiling.

Fire would introduce herself to Joy, her cheerless glossy lips downturned as she extends her hand to revealing long neon nails. "Hi, I'm Fire and this is Candy. We were Steve's favorite strippers. We miss him so much."

Then she would reminisce and share stories of my strip club adventures. "Once he ran over me in the booth and I was naked. He had a dirty mind but he couldn't fool me with his laugh."

"That's my brother," Joy would smile.

"Remember the time that wicked arm of his knocked a beer out of my arm, spilling beer on my outfit, including my panties." Candy steps back.

"That's Steve," Mary might say, laughing along with Patti and Kelly.

Fire's eyes would well as she told Joy, Mary, Patti, and Kelly. "I loved Steve. We dated but he wanted more. I just couldn't give him a relationship."

At the Silver Spoon, Fire takes my letter from an envelope taped to my knee. She reads it at the bar where the light is better. After she finishes reading the letter, she holds it with both hands close to her heart. "Let me check my calendar downstairs. I'll be right back."

I wait for her, feeling anxious and giddy.

Several minutes pass before she taps my shoulder. "I'd love to meet you there."

I'm flying high as a kite in the sky while I drink my beer

"I'm going downstairs to smoke. It's a nasty habit, I know. I'll be back." Fire touches my arm as she walked away.

I imagine what my female friends would say. I picture introducing Fire to my agent and being the talk of the writing conference. I fantasize about making love with her.

My readers are waiting for my next book. I want to be a New York author represented by a New York agent. I register for the writing conference at the Madison Concourse Hotel and reserve a room for the weekend.

I have spent weeks preparing for the weekend. Money from my trust fund paid for the hotel room and the conference. My daytime attendants from the Clove house were lined up. The manuscript was polished and I'd prepared an eight-minute speech to pitch to literary agents.

Until Paula says, "It isn't our job to accompany you at the hotel."

I feel defeated and I cry.

It's more than business or my career. The writing conference is camaraderie, being with novelists and essayists who understood the toil of writing. I am a valued member of this community, having attended the writing conference for twenty years. The conference is a place that I call "home" where I'm "Steve" not a cognitively disabled person.

After my mother passed, my writer friends supported me. My email dripped with my despair. I wanted to quit. I felt getting published was a pipe dream. They cheered me on. They convinced me my stories were important and readers would enjoy my books.

"Fuck you," I tell Paula. "I give up. I want to die. I have worked like hell. I'm sorry. I have to go to the conference. You figure it out. I want to watch TV in my office."

Paula wipes my eyes and the snot from my nose. "What channel do you want?"

"Sixty." She flips the TV to CNN and leaves. I listen to Wolf Blizter. For a while I fall asleep, escaping the mess as I hear my staff arguing about how to make the writing conference weekend work at the last minute. I'm tired. I close my ears resting my mind.

A knock at my door wakes me up. "Can I come in?" Brian, my counselor, stands in the doorway. He closes the door and takes a seat in my recliner. "Are you looking forward to the writing conference?"

"It'll be the last time I'll go." I break down crying again.

Brian holds me for a couple of minutes and after I calm down, he wipes my tears with a Kleenex. "Why do you say that?"

"I have to fight to take a shower, to go grocery shopping, have my fingernails cut, to travel, and the conference. I'm sick of it. I'm beginning my life. If I die tomorrow, I have nothing to be ashamed about. But I don't want to die."

"I understand." Brian pats me on my shoulder. "I'm sure that Jerry will make it happen."

I take a deep breath. "I'm tired Brian."

Brian nods.

Paula enters the room. "We've figured it out. You're going for the weekend, staying at the hotel. We can provide attendants at night."

Brian smiles at me.

My friends and writers come to my rescue. They volunteer as my daytime attendants during the conference. My agent is coming, I'm pitching a manuscript to Stephen King's agent, and Fire is coming for dinner. My date will be marzipan on a fudge torte.

I ask Paula to pack condoms in my suitcase. I'm ready to go.

The morning of the conference I'm up. Ralph is watching TV.

"Ajay, what is he doing up?" Ralph asks, sitting on the sofa.

"He is going to a hotel." Ajay makes pancakes in the kitchen.

"Why?" Ralph asks.

"I'm going home and to work." I look out of the window, waiting for the bus to arrive.

The sun shines through the bus windows as the bus driver picks up passengers. It feels strange to be up early. I'm impatient to get to the hotel and go to work.

"Cowboy, you ready to work?" the driver asks a man in a manual wheelchair, wearing a cowboy hat when the driver puts him on the lift in front of a green ranch house.

The man mutters something I can't hear and smiles at the driver.

We pick up another man, who rocks back and forth in his manual wheelchair. He screams each time the bus hits a bump.

I'm grateful that I don't have to deal with a morning bus ride like this every day.

Another nonverbal man gets on the bus with a teddy bear.

The driver heads downtown, stopping at the municipal county building, dropping off the cowboy, the screamer, and the teddy-bear man.

I wonder what the three men do at the courthouse. It doesn't matter. After the driver lets me off, he says, "Have a great day."

I enter the hotel and take a seat in the lobby.

My agent sees me. "You're here already."

"I have made it and I'll be here all weekend." I cry. The effort and fight to attend overwhelms me.

"You're among friends." Susan gives me a hug.

"I have got an idea for a new novel to talk to you about." I'm working before the conference even begins.

"Let's do lunch tomorrow."

I'm lucky I have an agent. My staff will never understand my passion and the love that people have for me. My dream of being a New York author is real. Each page that I write is one step closer towards reaching my dream.

I imagine going to New York, being interviewed by Good Morning America or the Today Show with a beautiful woman accompanying me. For a week I'm interviewed by the New York Post, Time, and the New York Times. A van shuttles me around the city, seeing the sights like Times Square, Statue of Liberty, and the World Trade Center. Of course, I see Madison Square Garden, the Barclays Center, Citi Field, Yankee Stadium, and Giants Stadium. At night I will see plays on Broadway with a beautiful woman. After the play we make love in a suite at the Trump Tower.

It takes countless emails and interviews to promote a book. Once I wrote a post for a podcast and answered a blog survey for a cerebral palsy organization all in one day. I'm here to sell my books, look for publicity opportunities, and network.

The first night I sit in the hotel lobby at 6:48 waiting for her. Arturo, my care attendant, is here. He made himself scarce. Time passes without any sign of Fire.

Have I been stood up?

A hotel receptionist asks me. "Are you Steven Salmon? Your dinner date is running late, but she's coming."

My heart flutters with her pending arrival. I envision us together in bed and my heart slams against my chest, bursting to get out.

My head, full with writing, distracts my racing pulse. For a few minutes I close my eyes, taking a cat nap. Hotel guests crisscross the lobby–muffled conversations surround me. Self-doubt creeps back. I fidget worrying that Fire might not show up.

Living in a group home should have taught me patience as I constantly wait for the attendants to aid me. Still, I hate waiting.

I have learned one thing about women is to be patient.

"Steve. Call me Roxy. Fire is my stage name."

I jumped when I heard Fire's voice. She wore a midnight blue dress that clung to her curvy hips, white high heels, and her hair curled across her breasts. "You're pretty tonight." The rocket has lifted off. My dream has turned into reality.

"I'm sorry I'm late. My daughter couldn't get in the house. I forgot to leave the key with her."

"Roxy, shall we go to the restaurant?" I test out her name. It feels foreign. We walk to the café and wait to be seated.

A waitress asked, "Table for two?"

"Can we have a table by the wall?" Roxy points to the table near the entrance.

The waitress moves chairs out of the way as I maneuvered my electric wheelchair to the table. She hands a menu to Roxy and places one on the table in front of me.

"Would you like to order a drink?"

Roxy peruses the menu. "Please give us some time."

"I'll be back." The waitress leaves us alone.

"Let's order wine instead of that Miller crap you drink."

I laugh as I scan the menu. My mind grapples with my reality—I'm on a date!

"Or," Roxy pauses for dramatic effect. "How about Sex on the Beach?"

Roxy's suggestion makes me laugh, a deep jagged rumble.

"Can get your mind out of the gutter? You're naughty."

I calm my body so I speak more clearly. "I want steak with blue cheese with roasted potatoes." Her perfume floats my way as she reaches for my menu.

"I'm ordering that, too." Roxy waves the waitress over. "We want two steaks with blue cheese with roasted potatoes and two Sex on the Beach. And please bring plenty of napkins and a straw."

I fill Roxy in on my day. "I got here before eight in the morning and worked all day. I have got a lead for an article, a podcast interview, and an offer to write another book for my agent. Tomorrow, I sell my books. Sunday, I'm on a panel with my agent, talking about a dream of a writer."

"You work so hard." Roxy gives me a sip of the cocktail.

"I'll be a New York author someday." I'm my biggest fan. Maybe Roxy will become one too.

"I believe in you." Roxy touches my arm and gives me another swig.

My care attendant, Arturo, taps my shoulder.

"This is Fire." I blush at my blunder and quickly correct. "Roxy."

They exchange pleasantries.

The waitress brings our steak dinners.

"It smells wonderful." Roxy looked at the sizzling steak. "I love to eat."

"Me, too." I take a bite with Arturo feeding me.

"You're here for the weekend?" Roxy asks, eating a mushroom.

"I am. The book signing is tomorrow and I have a meeting with my agent. Tell me more about yourself."

"Well, there isn't much to tell."

As my stomach fills, I worry about a bowel movement or vomiting my dinner if we go to bed too soon.

Roxy wipes off bits of blue cheese from my chin with a napkin. "There you are my dear."

"Roxy, would you go upstairs to my room with me?" Will my jetpack soar higher? I hold my breath.

"I would like to see your room, but no."

Crash and burn on descent. My heart shatters as the fantasy I built crumbles. My lower lip juts out.

"Don't give me your pouty face or I'll leave. I get enough of that from my daughter and I won't take it from you."

A mental shakedown adjusts my attitude. "I'm sorry."

"Apology accepted." Roxy pats my arm. "I'll stay for a little longer."

"Arturo I'll meet you in the bar later to go upstairs.

Take five dollars from my wallet to tip the waitress and put dinner on my hotel tab."

"You don't have to do that. I'll pay for it."

"I have got it. You've made my night special." I gaze into her eyes.

"Is your daughter a good cheerleader?" I forget my disappointment about not having sex with Roxy.

"She is. She twirls a flag and does cartwheels." Roxy smiles at me. "It has been difficult for us since I divorced my husband a year ago."

"I'm sorry. I know it is hard. When I was fourteen my Mom divorced after my Dad attempted suicide eight times in two years. The first time I was with him. I almost died."

When I was thirteen, my Dad was my hero. We did everything together from riding the lawn mower, watching him cut wood, tearing down walls, and building rooms. He even designed a tricycle for me. On weekends we traveled to the hardware store, the lumber company, tractor pulls, auctions, fairs, and carnivals.

"You're a survivor." Roxy caresses my long fingers in her hands.

I love her undivided attention.

Later in bed I replay the evening. "No Steve" keeps me awake. What is wrong with me? I wonder if any woman would marry me, considering my disability? What female wants a man, who drools, "dumps" in his pants, and gags on his food?

In junior high school my Special Education teacher,

Mr. Hart had severe Cerebral palsy. Mr. Hart could barely walk, drooled, and talked like me. He was married and had children. It was possible.

Why didn't Roxy want me? I refocus on our light conversation, her soft laugh, her rocking hard body. I press my naked body against the bed, imagining making love to Roxy. The magical evening permeates into my wet dream. Sleep comes upon me and I sleep for an hour.

I romanticize being an able-bodied man, showering with a woman, beads of water run down our bodies and the air heavy with steam and fogged mirrors, and then lie together on satin sheets in an extravagant hotel room. After I lost my virginity to Heather, I realized that sex was just that, sex.

I want a girlfriend to talk to, go out to eat with, and make love to. Someday I want a long-term commitment from a woman to spend the rest of my life with.

When the writing conference ends, it is back to Clove House. I have to return to my computer to start writing again. The glamour of the weekend lingers in my mind, but it is time to work. Being home means dealing with nonsense of my staff like being too busy to give me a shower for four days.

Friday following the conference, Fire gives me a lap dance at The Silver Spoon. During her break, she approaches me. "I read two of your books. They touched me and I think I understand you a little more. I want my daughter to meet you. You're a strong man. I truly mean that with the all of the shit that you have been through."

Fire's words touched my heart. She knew about my mother, the long hours of writing, the loneliness, and my determination.

I like to say that I'm burdock. The hook-bearing flowers become woody burrs and cling to fur and surfaces. They can be removed, but they pop back up if the roots are not completely dug and only to flourish even better than before. I have grown up through the last two years without my mother. She spoiled me, giving into my beck and call.

When I moved to Clove, I had to adjust to not being the center of attention. My attendants can say that I'm a self-centered person. It hurts, stopping me for a moment, but I return back stronger.

› DAD ‹

Dad operated a ham radio and taught me how to spell my name in Morse code. He took me to the ham radio club events. Dad had a sweet tooth for ice cream. He could eat a gallon in two days. Dad snuck candy bars, cookies, and donuts to me against Mom's rules about limiting how much sugar I should have.

I loved my Dad. In my eyes he couldn't do any wrong, but one morning it all changed.

It was time for me to have a haircut. We lived in southwestern Wisconsin out in the country with rolling hills, gravel roads, woods, and contour fields. Dairy farms dotted the majestic landscape.

Dad loaded me in the pickup truck and then secured my manual wheelchair in the truck's bed.

We headed to Leeds four miles away as I enjoyed the drive. Nothing seemed amiss. Dad made a U-turn back home when we reached Leeds and said, "I forgot something."

Dad sped around sharp curves and over hills, scaring me.

"Slow down, Dad."

Dad turned into a quarry. We passed the gravel pit used by the township to patch up the country roads. An aggregate company left a mountain of gravel for the town to pick up when needed.

Dad stopped and stared at a creek for a few minutes.

Cows chomped away at a round bale of hay, their tails swaying back and forth. After a while, I said, "Let's go home, Dad."

He drove behind the enormous pile of aggregate. We shouldn't be here. Alarm bells sounded in my head. He turned toward the pit.

I yelled, "No, Dad. Let's go see Mom."

Dad headed inside of the quarry, to the farthest end. He begun to drive up the mound. Dad reversed the pickup truck, and then ram it into the outcrop wall before rushing up the pile of gravel. He drove the truck up and down several times, frightening me.

"Stop, Buddy," I demanded. I waved my spastic arms to get his attention. Dad stopped the truck. "I want to go home. Now."

Dad's eyes didn't really focus on me even though he was staring at me. He was a refrigerator repairman. Dad reached behind the seat, grabbing a steel container of Freon. He pulled the trigger, spraying the cold grey foul-tasting gas at both of us.

I struggled to breathe. I vomited, urinated, and pooped in my pants.

Dad smacked me in the head with the Freon. My

body fell and crumpled under the dashboard. I lost unconsciousness.

A short time later my tight hamstrings spasm wakes me up.

"Buddy?" I couldn't read Dad's expression from the weird angle on the floorboard. I wanted to cry but I spoke softly to keep him calm. "Can I get up. Buddy?"

When Dad looked at me, I think this time he actually saw me. He lifted me onto the passenger seat and buckled my seat belt. Dad sat in silence, clutching the steering wheel. I was afraid to breathe.

Outside the passenger window I see the red, blue, white revolving cone, we were in front of a barber shop in Fend instead of Leeds. It was strange to be in another town.

"Buddy, I want to go to the hospital now." I didn't feel well, my body ached, and my clothes were stained with vomit and excrement. I needed help.

Dad nodded. His glazed eyes looked past me. I didn't feel he was really there. He drove out of Fend running a four-way stop.

"Buddy, I want a doctor." I was in shock. Tears rolled down my cheeks, but I kept calm to not upset Dad.

"I will." Dad drove back to the country.

"Dad! Go back. I want to go to the hospital."

Another quarry loomed ahead. Dad drove down a gravel road, passing dairy farms and fields. "I failed you. I'm sorry. Make a dent in the world because I haven't."

"I promise." I gripped my fingernails into the seat

while Dad drove faster. "Please stop. I have to pee." Maybe with this excuse I could get him to stop. My pants were soiled but almost dry.

Dad pulled over and walked to the passenger door, taking me in his arms. At a stand of woods, he pulled down my pants and undergarments, holding me against his body. He didn't notice or care that my pants were already messed. He zipped my jeans.

Carrying me back to the truck he stumbled and we fell to the ground. His weight pressed against me. He rolled off of me and dug in his pocket. He pulled out his pocketknife, unfolded it, and stared at it. The sun glinted off the blade.

He raised his arm, hesitated, before he jammed the blade in my chest. The pain jolted me and my body shuddered. I rolled onto my back to protect myself. I felt the blade slice into my back. I screamed for him to stop. When the blows stopped, I raised my head to look.

Dad was stabbing himself.

"Stop! Please Buddy. Stop!" I was crying.

He stopped. He sat on the ground next to me as if aware of what he had just done.

In between sobs, I said, "I need a doctor, Buddy."

Dad stood, picked me up, and walked to the pickup truck. After he fastened my seat belt, Dad raced off. I sat in the passenger seat, believing we would have help soon. Instead Dad careened into an embankment, tipping over the truck several times before it landed on its roof. I came to, dangling by my seatbelt. Tiny rainbows danced as the sunlight refracted off the spider-cracked windshield. Dad was silent. It seemed for a really long time.

A passing motorist arrived after the accident. "Are you okay?"

"I think," I said. Blood dripped onto the ceiling of the car. As I waited for rescue, I struggled to comprehend what took place. I knew my Dad loved me but why did he do this?

At home, after I was discharged from the hospital, Mom tried to explain depression. Dad did love me, but he was sick. Dad survived but he never recovered from his depression. Four months later I forgave him but he couldn't forgive himself. It wasn't until I was much older that I understood his hopelessness.

His words: "Make a dent in the world," stuck in my mind throughout my life.

When I want to give up, when everything seems hopeless, especially after Mom passed, I keep moving on to the next challenge. Being an author, who lives in a group home, presents its share of problems but I manage.

› LIFE ‹

I visit the strip club on Fridays when I knew Fire is working. I want a second date with her. The lap dances aren't enough. My connection to her is more than her giving me a beer, making small talk, and dancing on the stage.

She winks, blows kisses, and stares at me. I imagine Fire likes my company.

She gave me her email address but she didn't reply to my email, making me wonder if I made a mistake. I wait for her to email me. It hurts me. What to do? I'm a lonely man, pursuing his first woman. Should I call her?

My work distracts me and I forget about Fire. Book publicity takes off with two major articles coming in succession of each other, a book signing at Barnes & Noble, and papers waiting for critique.

A reporter and a photographer from the Wisconsin State Journal shot pictures of me, tapping Morse code. My attendants like the photo and the article, but when I ask them to take copies of the memoir to the bookstore the answer is, "I don't have time."

I email my friend, Paul, who takes the books to the bookstore.

I need attendants to assist me with my personal care for special events or travel. When I want to visit my four college classmates or attend the writing conference, Paula tells me, "That isn't our job. We just take care of you."

"I give up. Fuck you. I want to die."

When I have a career opportunity like a book signing, I needed some extra help from my staff. The answer was "No." I would say, "I'll kill myself," trying to get my attendants to do what I want. I have said this all of my life to get my way, including with Mom and my sister, Joy. When things seem hopeless, I will say it. Of course, I don't act upon it, but I think about it until I move forward. Right now, I feel beaten. Care attendants should be hired to assist me with my life, to live life.

"I'll call Jerry and he'll put you under suicide watch, meaning you can't go anywhere," Paula threatens.

The first couple years at Clove, I did say, "I'm killing myself," often to have what I wanted. I didn't want my freedom be taken away, but at the time I was expressing my anger.

"I'm not going to the book signing. I want to write." I take a deep breath, calming myself.

Paula pushes me into my office.

I write another post for my blog as I listen to my attendants bicker on the phone about me.

During the summer I spend my time writing interviews, signing books at Barnes & Noble, and composing another book. I avoid the strip club after Fire rejected me. After I gave Fire twenty dollars for a cab to meet me at Starbucks, she stood me up. I was hurt.

I email Heather for sex. Lying next to her, smelling her alcoholic breath, turns my stomach. I pay her sixty dollars for five minutes and realize I am throwing my money away.

"Thanks. This will help pay my car note." Heather takes the cash from the radio before walking out of my bedroom.

I had more fun at the strip club drinking beer, ogling naked women, watching sports on Al's new big screen TV, than sex with Heather. Dances with Fire were twenty dollars and the conversations were free. Plus, Fire made sure I received my share of attention.

The last time at the club Fire told me, "I have got to get a new email address. I'm working on it. You'll be the first to have it." Then she winked at me.

A month later I visited The Silver Spoon hoping get a second date and so I wrote a letter to her that read:

Roxy,

Please meet me at the Memorial Union this Sunday at two for ice cream on the UW Credit Union Stage. Also, I'm going to a wedding party for an old care attendant in Keen next Saturday. I hired a cab to take me. Are you interested in going? Roxy, I'm independent now, but it hurts to go out alone seeing couples together. I want a female friend to go out with sometimes. Nothing serious. No pressure.

Steve

At the club she reads my letter. "Yes, to Sunday, but I have got to check my calendar about next Saturday." Fire kisses my forehead.

I'm soaring high as she walks back to work. The ruckus it would cause at the wedding if Fire came with me. What would my sister and my three women friends from college say? In my imagination, my best friend from up north, Lisa, would confront me the next day at my house, demanding details.

With shock in her voice she might say, "Dating a stripper and the hooker!" She'd playfully bop me on my head.

I'd laugh picturing me sitting at my mother's grave, talking to Mom. "I'm a real author with two new published books but I can't help the women and the beer. It's my life now. I love it."

Fire walks by again. "I make really good spicy spaghetti and garlic bread. Maybe I'll make that for you sometime."

For several minutes I dream we're sitting on the patio of her house. She's feeding me pasta, chicken, a tossed salad and garlic bread. We drink wine that I brought in her lush backyard with a garden of sunflowers. A light breeze blows as fire flies light up here and there. I can eat all that I want unlike at home.

She kisses me while the sun sets. Fire holds my hand in hers. We sit, listening to the crickets.

I'm in love. The evening is tranquil but nothing is that easy. At that moment I can envision the possibilities.

The dream ends.

The bus driver stands at the door, waiting to take me home. In the driveway, I gaze up at the stars in the sky, making a wish. I brace myself for endless complaining, backstabbing, and fighting for my rights as I enter Clove house.

› NONSENSE ‹

When I lived with my mother, I had seconds and even thirds of helpings of food. My mother often made pork or beef roast with potatoes, carrots, rutabaga, and onions with homemade gravy. I enjoyed eating tomatoes and cucumbers with my meal. For dessert she piled raspberries over vanilla ice cream. She heaped my plate with the first helping and fed me until I was stuffed.

My mother risked that it could come right back up. One time I finished Thanksgiving dinners only to throw up in front of my entire family. My loud-mouthed cousin, Larry, helped clean my mess at my grandparent's house saying "This isn't that bad, not like puking Taco Bell all over my truck while I'm driving seventy miles per hour down the interstate after the Brewers game."

My family laughed as my mother fed me again.

When my jaws locked open during a meal, she'd say in a loud voice, "Control, Steve."

I hated hearing those two words. Over the years, my vomiting became worse. The last years of my mother's life I threw up frequently and didn't leave the house much.

It only happens occasionally now. I'm able to go out after supper without vomiting. If I do vomit it's usually at home. It drives me crazy when Teresa gives a single potato, a small serving of green beans, and a drumstick for dinner.

"I want one more potato please," I say.

"You've had enough. I'm not cooking anymore." Teresa glares a dirty look at me and walks to the sofa to sit down.

The next day Paula dumps the potato I would have eaten had Teresa prepared it because it is tiny and moldy. Then she calls me wasteful.

At that moment I'm helpless and powerless until I'm seated at the computer.

Overnight an attendant, Nedie, says, "I'm not staying up all night for you to write. I'm tired. You're full of yourself. No one cares about you. You can't do anything."

"Go to hell. I'm an author. People love me and people who I don't know care about me."

"No one even loves you. Someone has to wipe your ass. Now go to bed." Nedie stays seated on the sofa.

Her attempts to demean me hit home, but outwardly I act nonchalantly. "I do what I want and I'll go to bed when I want." I continue watching SportsCenter checking the baseball scores.

"You're selfish. That's why you're alone. No one even likes you. I have got a headache." Nedie puts her index finger to her mouth.

Once I get on the computer, I will email Jerry telling him of the verbal abuse and being denied my access to write. It is not that easy to remove a care attendant from a house. I might have to write several emails to get them out of Clove. Then Integration has to find a replacement, taking more time. There is a sediment at Integration I send emails to get attention. I have learned to send emails to Jerry when it is absolutely necessary. Eventually I have my way.

"Fuck you." I thrash my arms.

"You're going to hell." Nedie gets down on her knees to pray for me. "Forgive him, God he doesn't know what he says."

The feeling of depression floods my mind while thoughts of suicide haunt me. I rarely see my family and friends. My mind tricks me into thinking that I'm not loved.

I send an email to my love ones who cares, receiving love from everywhere. So many people love me now, from my friend, Doug at Sal's, to writers, and of course the staff at the strip club.

Another evening at The Silver Spoon Fire assists me with my beer. "I don't want to go home. They say I'm an awful person. I'm evil and don't want to go to bed early."

"They don't know who you are." Fire stares into my eyes.

I know who I am. The staff can't take that away from me. My dream of being a well-known author is slowly becoming true.

It took me eight years to land a literary agent and another three years to write a middle-grade book.

I fought to write two books while adapting to life in a group home after losing my mother. Day and night, I wrote. Fourteen months after the death of my mother I published my books. Now six months after being published I'm working with my agent to have a book signing at Barnes & Noble.

"It is the book signing, you people!" I sound like an angry teacher, scolding a class. My attendants hate being called, "You people."

"Sorry, I'm busy." The same answer, leaving me to email my friend, Bob.

Five minutes later, Kerry walks into my office. "I'll take the books to the store Saturday."

"Thank you, but I have a friend picking up the books."

It is always the same struggle with my attendants when I get an opportunity to promote my books or I want to travel, but without an attendant, I can't. When I make plans to visit my college classmates up north or attend a three-day writing conference, I get the same response, "I'm busy."

Tawania says to Teresa, "I can't wait to go on vacation next month to Atlanta. And I need a vacation. I work so hard."

"Girl, I'm taking my vacation on Friday for two weeks. I'm getting the hell out of here." Teresa is frying a hamburger on the stove.

I work harder and longer than any of my attendants

except for Kerry, who is a workaholic, managing four houses, doing On Call, and putting up with me.

Writing fourteen hours every day takes a toll on an author. I need to go away, too. Demands, deadlines, and the never-ending problems with care become too much at times.

When Fire calls Candy over, I'm sitting at the bar. "Candy, come over and hear what Steve's attendants say about him."

Candy walks over to me. "Let's hear it."

It lightens my mood when I say it in front of friends who know it's not true. "I'm evil and no one cares about me."

Star goes behind the bar, taking a flexible straw from a plastic bag. A simple gesture like this tells me people cares about me. She replaces the regular straw with the bendable one. "I bought these for Steve to make it easier for him to drink."

"Isn't that ridiculous?" Fire gives me another swig of beer. "And he doesn't want to go home. What are we going to do with you?"

I picture the three strippers as my care attendants. I'd go home to them in a New York minute.

I'm independent now. It frustrates me when my attendants don't do what I want or need.

"Nedie, please cook chicken, potatoes, and peas for supper." I'll say, leaving soon to spend the entire afternoon at the Memorial Union.

"That's the p.m. shift job." Nedie remains on the sofa.

"Please tell Teresa to make it."

"No, I'm tired," Nedie says, yawning.

I don't argue with her. The bus arrives taking me to the Union to escape Clove house. I sleep and think for most of the afternoon, knowing that there won't be anything to eat when I go home. I'm hungry now. I go inside the Union. "I want a pizza."

The clerk behind the counter is puzzled. "What?"

A short order cook butts in. "He wants pizza. What kind of pizza do you want, sir?"

"Pepperoni." I'm grateful when people take the time and show the patience to understand my wants.

"What size do you want?"

"Medium."

"That's eight dollars."

"I have money in the back." I motion my head towards the back of the wheelchair.

He walks from the counter over to me. "Where's your money?"

"In my wallet, in the small pocket of the bag." I shake my head to the back again.

He digs through the backpack and pulls out my wallet, but the zipper won't open. Somehow, he gets my debit card out. "Can I use your card?" He runs the card through the cash register. Then he put the card back in the wallet and returns it to the backpack. "Your order will be ready shortly."

"Thank you." My right shoe falls off.

A woman asks, "Can I put your shoe back on?"

"Yes, please." I watch her, putting my shoe back on.

The cook brings the pizza on a tray. "Where do you want the pizza?"

"Box the pizza and put it in my bag, please."

He shuffles things around to make it fit. When he finishes, he says, "You're good to go."

When I get home, Teresa asks, "What are you eating for dinner?"

"Pizza is in the bag. Please heat it up. Thank you." I take great satisfaction in knowing I can do things on my own.

A couple of days earlier, I went to Sal's and I forgot to ask Nedie to douse me with bug spray. It's my responsibility to remind my attendants what I need before I leave Clove house, but on this particular day I woke up late. The bus was here. If I'm not out within five-minute window, the bus leaves without me. I had no time to have her spray me and I didn't want to miss my ride. The mosquitoes bit me as I boarded the bus. After I arrive downtown, I go to Walgreens to buy bug spray. I flag down a clerk to help me. "Can you help me?"

He follows me through the narrow aisles to the bug spray.

"I want Off, green bottle." I gesture with my eyes to the top shelf.

"This one?" The clerk holds it in front of me.

I have a difficult time, maneuvering the wheelchair down the aisle. "I have money in my wallet in the bag on the back of the wheelchair."

"You don't have to pay."

"I'll pay." I navigate the aisles to the cash register.

The clerk retrieves my wallet out of the bag when I arrive at the counter.

"Can you spray me, please?"

The clerk sprays my arms, legs, hands, neck, ears, and face at the counter.

"Thank you for all of your help. I greatly appreciate it."

Being independent sometimes require my determination and the help of kind strangers.

I have a scheduled ride to go downtown, but it is forecasted to rain tonight. "Paula, please cancel the bus." I was stuck in a thunderstorm once. The electric wheelchair didn't move, leaving me stranded.

"You shouldn't be canceling all of these rides. They'll take away your service."

Paula is watching a movie on her tablet.

"They'll cancel your service if you keep canceling rides."

Jimmy is watching *Green Acres* on TV.

"Cancel the bus." It irritates me when I have to repeat myself.

"I'll cancel the bus, but you need to plan your activities better." Paula moves slowly to the phone, annoyed she has to move.

Next time I'll consult my weather-predicting crystal ball before scheduling any future events. A shower pours at seven while I watch the Brewers in bed, safe and dry.

The sound of the rain makes me sleepy. Thunder follows the flash of light. The wheelchair is ready for my next outing rather than having an electrical short that would need to repair.

As recommended by my dentist, I schedule my annual physical three weeks prior to having my teeth cleaned. I email my care agency's nurse to make an appointment with my doctor.

When the wheelchair needs a repair or an adjustment it's my sole job to email the vendor and schedule service. Matt is coming tomorrow to fix my head array. One of my care attendants knocked it off center making it hard to drive my electric wheelchair. I rely on others to safeguard my equipment. Sometimes, when it gets damaged, it is out of my control.

Medicaid pays for limited repair visits after that I am financially responsible.

One mid-afternoon I emailed Matt asking him to come to adjust the head array this week. I received his answer a couple of minutes later, saying, "I'll be there tomorrow at ten."

The next morning, I wake up at nine. "Hey, hey, hey."

Ajay knocks and opens the door. "Yes, author?"

"Get up."

"But it's early." Disbelief is written on his face. "Paula isn't here. I can't give you a shower." Ajay pats me on my shoulder.

"I have an appointment." I would rather sleep, but I'm an adult.

"I'll give you a bed bath."

I'm quiet as Ajay washes, dresses, and lifts me in his muscular arms, putting me in the manual wheelchair. I am ready when Matt arrives carrying his toolbox to fix the head array.

My decisions are now bigger and more important than buying a birthday cake for my mother. My attendants take my independence for granted or see it as a nuance. I forward emails to Paula or Kerry with an address, asking to schedule a ride to a specific place. An email provides proof of my request. I could have verbalized the address but I don't remember the zip code. At the time Kerry and Paula were on the phone and it is easier to shoot an email, avoiding an argument.

I don't answer, choosing to ignore her. I continue to write.

When I go to the playwrights meeting, I'm among creative minds, who give me inspiration, seeing other writers, listening to plays, and making me want to write a play myself. Afterwards we walk a couple of blocks to a bar to have a drink and talk shop.

A member of the group, Gene, says, "It's hard to get a review in the Wisconsin State Journal, The Isthmus, or Madison Magazine these days."

"The Isthmus wrote a review for my play, *A New Time,* being produced next week at the Bartell Theater." Eric says, sipping a beer.

I'm eating up the conversation since I have feature articles in the Wisconsin State Journal and Madison Magazine in two weeks. I know how hard publicity is. It reminds me how far I have come and to continue moving forward.

I return home after eleven when the overnight attendant, Marty says, "You shouldn't be out so late and now I have to transfer you alone. You need to get back by ten."

"I do what I want. I'm not Jimmy."

"You don't need to be out at this time of night." Marty uses the Hoyer lift, transferring me from the electric wheelchair to the manual wheelchair. "I don't know if I can do this. Where were you tonight?"

Writers are a breath of fresh air for me. We practice mental exercises, crafting our ideas, composing our stories, of which I am on the same playing field as them.

No writer should be told to come home early, have to argue to eat ice cream, be denied a shower, or be patient to use the bathroom, until they decide it's convenient for them.

Sunday, one care attendant is here. Jimmy is sound asleep in bed. Nothing is prepared for supper. I'm hungry, thirsty, and tired. I want to nap. My butt hurts. I need to pee.

Lisa is on the cell phone, talking to her boyfriend and smoking. I get her attention to help me with the urinal, but she forgets to cook supper. Then Lisa starts my chicken before going back to the front step to smoke.

"Call Kerry and tell her to get over here now." I'm angry expecting a meal waiting for me.

I want to go back into the world, living like the panhandlers down on State Street rather than being home.

STEVE
ISN'T HOME

After a wonderful evening, I return home to Tawania saying, "Email your cousin Larry about whether you're taking a cab tomorrow to Rockford or should he pick you up for your aunt's memorial."

"Call him now."

"It's late. He's asleep like normal people are." Tawania crosses her arms, daring me to ignore social norms and common courtesy.

"Larry is a night owl like me. Get my address book and call."

"I won't call him."

"Tawania, it's important."

She finds Larry's number and punches it into the receiver.

"If he doesn't answer, I'm not calling again." She holds the phone to my ear.

After the second ring, Larry picks up. "Hello."

"Larry, I can't get a cab. It is too late. Please come and get me."

"I'll be there at eleven. You were at the club again, right?" Larry laughs.

"It's Saturday night and you know me. It's my life now. I was going go to the Memorial Union tomorrow, but I'll cancel those plans."

"You're never home, nonfiction writer," Larry says, making fun of my genre since I only write what I know.

"You mean author." I know I'm right, but Larry must have the last word.

"Whatever, writer with no imagination, I can write a book in a month. Nonfiction writer, I'll see you today at eleven. Good night," Larry says, yawning before he hangs up.

The days of calling the day before a family gathering—and expecting me to be there—are long gone. Cabs need to be arranged in advance and cost a lot of money even for a short distance. My service agency pays for a cab to visit my sister, Joy and two nieces in Milwaukee on Thanksgiving, Christmas, and Easter. If I want to go somewhere outside of Madison, I rent a van or pay for a cab out of my own pocket.

After my mother passed away, I thought about keeping my wheelchair accessible van with a ramp to visit my four friends from college every fall and also travel to different places. My sister and I decided to sell the van. The sixteen-year-old van needed realignment, body work, and the insurance was sky-high for a third-party driver.

There was nowhere to park the van at my new home other than the street. The garage was filled with discarded medical equipment and boxes. My attendants parked in the driveway.

Before my mother died, I was always on the computer, emailing people and writing.

After being on my own, I needed time away from Clove house. It started slowly, but on the first anniversary of my mother's death, I was going out almost daily. I didn't know what I was looking for at the time. I felt lost. Was there more to life than writing? Something was missing but I couldn't put my finger on it. I wanted to share my life with other people.

Writing is my passion. Losing my mother, adjusting to living in a group home, becoming an adult, and writing two books make me tired. Being out gives me the strength to battle onward, but this is all new to my family.

I sit by the window waiting for Larry. I'm looking forward to seeing my sister, Joy and my cousins Ray, Gina, Andy, and Jill, who all live out West. This might be the last time that I see them.

I want to tell my family about my new life.

Ray, Larry, and I are about the same age, separated by only six months. I want to share my first experience being with a woman with my two cousins. Everything is so new and I can't wait to go to Rockford.

The clock ticks past eleven. Jimmy is asleep in his electric wheelchair, watching *The Brady Bunch*. Time keeps passing. My bus parks in the street. It is noon.

What if Larry doesn't make it? I don't want to be in Clove house. "Tawania, did you call to cancel my ride?"

"I did." Tawania leans across me to look out the window.

"I'll take the bus. Please put me in the power chair." Disappointment creeps into my voice.

Nedie and Tawania transfer me to the electric wheelchair, but Tawania asks, "Don't you think that you should wait?"

"I'm going." I drive out the door to the bus.

The dispatcher radios the driver when we are halfway to the Union saying, "Your twelve o'clock pick up Steven Salmon is canceled."

"Steven is on the bus now and I'm taking him to the Memorial Union," the driver tells the dispatcher.

"Ten four," the dispatcher says.

I hope that means my pick-up time at Memorial Union is still valid. I feel like a child running away from their parents, hiding where the parents know where the kid is.

It was stupid to not wait for Larry. I should have called him to see where he was. I often had to wait for Larry when we traveled or did something together.

Part of me wanted to rebel, to show my family I'm making my own decisions. Would my family wonder why I didn't attend her celebration of life? Would they ask why Larry showed up late without me?

I'm being selfish. I should have waited.

I need to go. I don't know why. When I arrive at the

Memorial Union, I drive to the second terrace. I park in the middle in front of the stage, watching the sail boats glide across the water. Puffy white clouds float in the clear blue sky.

Talking to myself, "Well, Aunt May goodbye. You were a great woman, who never complained or wanted anything. You just wanted family, but we were too busy to visit you, including me. Mom and you are together now. Mom, Dad, Uncle Jay, Uncle Fred, and you are gone. Life is new for me with women and beer. Mom wouldn't like it, I know. A man has needs. I miss Mom. I love you. Amen."

It hurts, missing my family. Do they miss me? The opportunity to be together happens rarely. I imagine them eating submarine sandwiches, potato chips, vegetables with French onion dip, and homemade cookies. My mouth waters thinking about double chocolate chip cookies. Who would eulogize my Aunt May's life?

In the back of my mind I'm in trouble for not attending. I picture my family talking about me afterwards. Larry would put the blame on me.

I love my family. Our careers and lives are fast paced. I know that my family and friends think about me.

› JIMMY ‹

I'm in the office, emailing a writer. The doorbell rings. "I'm here to see Jimmy. I'm Chad, his brother." He rustles down the hall to Jimmy's bedroom. I overhear their mundane conversation.

"Hi, Chad. How's it going?" Jimmy asks, chuckling.

"Pretty good. Happy Birthday. Sixty-two, that's ancient!" Chad exclaims.

"I am. I went to Catholic Charities today. We had pot roast, mashed potatoes with gravy, carrots, and apple sauce. It was good. I played checkers with Chester. We played Wheel of Fortune and Bingo. And I won another ape in Bingo," Jimmy says.

He's probably showing off the stuffed brown monkey, hanging on the wall near the fish tank.

"That's great. I have something for you," Chad says.

The bag crinkles. "Two T-bone steaks and baked beans."

"Thank you. Teresa and I are going to Outback Steakhouse tonight. I'm going to have a New York strip, a baked potato with bacon bits, and a hot fudge sundae with peanuts with whipped cream."

"Cancel the ice cream sundae. Your blood sugar is 180 and you've got the runs. I hate cleaning up messes. No sweets, my dear," Kerry says.

"Okay, my darling," Jimmy says.

"Chocolate shake tomorrow if your blood sugar is low. I'll get it myself and pay for it." Kerry voice becomes clearer as she walks into the hall.

"I have to go, Jimmy."

"Thank you for the steak and the beans."

Chad visits Jimmy every couple of months and he doesn't stay long. He calls Jimmy once a week. Their conversations center around the food they ate that day. No one else comes to see Jimmy.

No matter what shift it is Jimmy greets any female care attendant by calling, "Come here, my darling." He can be sound asleep, but he knows who is working and the time of the shift.

Jimmy enjoys making small talk with the staff. "So, Kerry, you're doing a double shift tonight."

"No one wanted to work today for some reason. Jerry will have my head; Integration is worried about overtime. Yes, I'm working sixteen hours."

"That's unfair, my darling." Jimmy goes back to sleep.

I'm jealous of Jimmy. The staff babies him.

When I want or need something, I have to wait, but it feels like the staff is always there when Jimmy calls. I have responsibilities and a career he doesn't.

If I complain, "I'm a bad guy," but Jimmy is a perfect angel. I expect my laundry to be done and my needs met in a timely manner unlike Jimmy, who is a kind gentleman, living a simple life.

Jimmy and I don't talk much. He is hard of hearing and my poor speech makes it difficult for us to have a conversation, but we both love the Packers and ice cream.

"The Packers play the Vikings on Monday Night Football. I can't wait to see it." Jimmy drinks coffee from a Packer plastic mug.

"It's a big game. The defense needs more help, but we'll win."

Jimmy is asleep when I leave for Sal's to watch the game with Doug.

I need to go pee.

Jimmy wakes up when I get home. He checks the score on the local news.

"Jimmy, did the Packers win?" Ralph asks, eating lunch the next day.

"The Packers won 28 to 21. Kerry, I want ice cream."

"What was your blood sugar?" Kerry asks.

"It's 182." Jimmy licks his lips.

"Your blood sugar is still too high. Tomorrow, if your blood sugar is lower, I'll buy you a milkshake from Culvers." Kerry touches his arm.

"Okay, my dear," Jimmy says.

I feel sorry for Jimmy. When I see how little he has, it makes me want to live life to the fullest.

Both of us love food, women, are in wheelchairs, and

need twenty-four-seven assistance. There are many differences between us. He receives an "allowance" of fifty dollars a week that he uses to order take-out. Jimmy was a happy-go-lucky guy, who doesn't ask for much.

I often wondered what happened to his wife. My imagination concocted two scenarios. I imagined that after becoming disabled and moving into a nursing home his wife divorced him. The other scenario was that he asked her to leave him as he felt no longer useful by not being able to walk. This was very possible given Jimmy's selflessness.

"Tawania, baby." Jimmy smiles at her. "I'm paying for dinner."

"Jimmy, it's your birthday. I'm paying for it."

"No, darling. Let me pay." Jimmy opens his arms for a hug.

Sometimes I wish I have the same kind of relationships with my care attendants.

› DREAMS ‹

Two months after my mother passed away, I was still numb and adjusting to my new life when I asked Jerry to take Lindy to the vet.

"You're taking my cat in and I'll go with you."

I miss the days when my mother did everything.

Everything was so new. Each day offered a different challenge I had to solve. As we waited for the bus, Lindy meowed from within the animal carrier on the side of the curb.

Jerry asked, "What are you going to do with the rest of your life?"

"Get published and become a New York author."

"Do you want to get married and have kids?"

I laughed, thinking about being "ridden" several times until I couldn't ejaculate.

Having kids wasn't in my mind even though I like children. I couldn't afford them much less take care of them. I dream of falling in love with a woman and maybe marrying her. She would be special, a lady who sees beyond the drool and the wheelchair.

I was learning how to live without my mother, handling my business, adapting to a staff who takes care of me, and writing books. I write fourteen hours a day. Being published was what I wanted. I desired to have a female companion.

Loneliness set in. I took naps to forget about my worries.

I lived an isolated life with my mother. Except for my birthday, we didn't go out to eat very often. We spent our days reading, writing, emailing, and watching sports on TV at night. I stayed inside most of the time writing.

Mom forbade drinking, going to the strip club, or driving my electric wheelchair downtown alone.

Once, Larry and I stayed out late. Mom asked, "Where have you two been? The Brewers game was over at ten. It is two in the morning."

I knew we would be in trouble for making Mom stay up into the wee morning hours. I didn't resist Larry's tempting offer coming back from Milwaukee.

"Let's go to the strip club on East Washington Avenue and have some fun."

I put up a mild fuss. It was late. I needed my muscle relaxation medicine.

"Live a little. The night is yours." Larry pulled into the parking lot of the strip club.

I felt excited in the dark place with flashing lights while loud music plays and men sit in black chairs, watching a woman twirl on a pole. It was the first time seeing naked women. The stirring in my pants embarrassed me.

"Now don't stare until they look at you." Larry gave me a sip of Coke while he drank a beer.

I enjoyed having breasts in my face, watching the dancers dance, and getting smiles from gorgeous women. My worry about Mom slipped away, replaced by the female attention. Going home could wait.

"Answer me, Steven," Mom demanded.

"The strip club." I yawned.

Mom's jaw dropped. Larry stepped in the bedroom doorway. "He's going to sleep good tonight with a lot of sweet dreams."

Ten years have passed and I'm a regular at the strip club. Seeing naked women does not excite me as much anymore. I watch the game on the big screen TV, drinking, and waiting for Fire to arrive. After the romantic dinner at the Concourse Hotel, having a lap dance with Fire didn't matter to me.

After having sex a few times with Heather, sex isn't what I want. I wanted a girlfriend.

I have had crushes but not a relationship. My three female college classmates were like sisters. I could talk to them about anything, including sex which they didn't want to hear.

Sometimes I didn't know what I was doing living with my mother for seventeen years after graduating from college. We lived in a condominium for twelve years in the outskirts of Madison. I didn't know how to get around downtown. I would go to the Concert on the Square with my friend, Bob.

In April I attend the annual three-day writing conference which was the highlight of my year. My friends met me in the lobby to help me with writing notes and pitching manuscripts to literary agents, but my mother would pick me up at five.

Mom grocery-shopped and went to the Sherman Avenue neighborhood farmers' market before I was up. "I would go to the farmers' market downtown to buy Bing cherries, but I don't want to deal with parking," Mom told my friend Bob once.

Here I am strolling down the square, getting vegetables and Door County cherries.

Paula will tell me when I get home, "You shouldn't buy cherries since I have to pit them."

It's part of the job taking care of me.

Sitting on the terrace at the Memorial Union on a beautiful summer afternoon, looking at the Pyle Center reminds me how far I have come. Yet, I want to return home to the condominium with my mother.

I wake up at noon, working until five in the morning, doing publicity for my books.

It's lunchtime at Clove house. Jimmy needs his blood sugar check and insulin.

Ralph comes home from work. Ralph and Jerry are hungry. Paula cooks their meals. Ajay is helping her.

After lunch, it's Paula's lunchtime. She goes to get take-out.

My showers didn't happen. Paula said to me after missing a fourth day without a shower, "You need to go to bed earlier at night. We are not giving showers at noon."

I emailed Jerry about not showering.

An hour later, Kerry walks in the office with an angry look, throwing her arms in the air. "You lied to Jerry that you hadn't had a shower for four days."

"It is true."

"All that you do is email Jerry."

"You've got no idea what I do each day." I tap Morse code at the computer.

"I hate it that you're your own guardian." Kerry gives me a dirty look.

I went to a lawyer about four months before my mother's death, shifting the power of attorney to me. My foresight of seeing my mother, becoming forgetful and fragile caused me to take a few steps of empowerment, protecting my ability to make decisions for myself.

At the time I was thinking about the future not knowing that my mother was going to die soon. If I hadn't become my own guardian, I would have become a ward of the state.

Now I have the freedom to do what I want, like going out at night or staying up until three in the morning. My attendants can try to tell me to come home before ten to do a second-person transfer, but I actually have no curfew. When I want or need money, Kerry withdraws it from my bank. I drink responsibly, don't get into trouble, and I stay where I tell Paula to have the bus pick me up instead of taking off for somewhere else.

Kerry confronts me one day. "Will you stop making trouble telling Jerry that you didn't have supper last night because Tawania got mad at you?"

"That's a lie. You were being argumentative with me and the bus came to take you to that hole in the wall to see Fire or Roxy." Tawania wipes the dining room table with a paper towel.

"I asked to get up at five, but you waited until 5:45 to get me. I need to eat because I'm going to drink and if I don't eat, I will get acid reflux." I'm stating the truth.

"You want a girlfriend, but your attitude stinks. No woman will want you if that's the way you treat your female staff." Kerry points her index finger at me.

I don't like hearing that my attitude is horrible. I'm not mellow like Jimmy or always happy like Ralph. A few of my attendants expect me to act like my roommates. I have many feelings. I'm tough, but I can be very sensitive.

My career demands a lot of me. An author has to be a professional with his agent, publishers, the news media, and readers. I have to make compromises with my staff, but I have to be assertive at times with some of my attendants, making my point.

I am a loyal hard-working man, who cares what people think about me. I like my roommates and staff, but I avoid them by sleeping in the morning or working in my office.

An author needs a place to create and think.

"I know that you want your own apartment, but your income isn't enough to afford the rent." Jerry is sitting on a park bench. "I want you to be happy. I'll keep looking, but you'll need a roommate and you probably won't have an office."

Either I have too much money or not enough according to the system. I'm a part-time teaching assistant for a speech instructor at a technical college, making three hundred dollars a year, critiquing papers. I earn sixty dollars a year from my books. I'm a full-time author, working over forty hours a week.

Writing is a complicated long process, requiring an office to write.

I feel stuck living with my roommates and their simple lives. I don't want to just write all of the time. There will be a girlfriend someday.

I imagine bringing a woman to my apartment after a date, making love in the shower.

Dreams keep me alive, pushing me to the normal American dream with a place of my own and a woman. Will I ever be happy?

› Life Is Good ‹

"Life is good." All my writer friends tell me this in their emails, reminding me how far I have come in the two years since my mother passed. "You're making it. Two books published, major articles written, and podcasts. We wish that we can do what you do."

I worry that I will fail. In the back of my mind I know that I have succeeded, but I also want to be more widely known.

Fire taps me on my shoulder. "Al texted me that you were here. Where's your envelope?"

I didn't expect to see Fire on a Sunday knowing she spends weekends with her daughter. I didn't write her a letter, planning to have a dance with Candy or another dancer at halftime.

"I came to work just for you. You had your dance, I see. I have told you to wait for me until I got here." She walks away.

I turn on the electric wheelchair to follow Fire. I wait next to the stairwell, as I watch the game. Why do women make everything hard?

Fire approaches me. "I had two cube steaks on the grill and I came in on my day off."

"I have got money." I imagine eating supper with her.

"I'm on next." Fire moves a chair so I can watch her dance.

I park the wheelchair in the middle of the club where I can keep one eye on the game and the other on her.

Aaron Rodgers makes short passes, taking the Packers down the field at the end of the second quarter.

Fire hunches down in front of me. I'm having a difficult time, concentrating on both.

Fire struts away and rubs against another man.

I'm realizing that she isn't interested in me, period. I don't want to believe it. I go back to the bar to drink and watch the second half of the game.

"Where's the money?" Fire asks.

"In the backpack in my wallet." I feel her dig around in my bag.

Fire opens my wallet in front of me but doesn't find the money

"Keep looking."

The cash is hidden in a pocket with my debit card. She takes out forty dollars to pay for the beer and asks Al for the change. Fire puts the money in the wallet, then back in the bag. "Meet me in the back corner."

A couple of months ago another man in an electric wheelchair clipped a hinge of a booth, breaking the swinging doors.

Al mandated lap dances to men in wheelchairs should be in the corner.

Business owners are running a business and are not care attendants, but it is a part of my life now. I maneuver the wheelchair to the corner.

"A little more."

I inch forward.

"That's good."

I press my chin on the power switch, turning off the wheelchair.

Fire hesitates looking around at who is watching. "I don't like this. Doing a dance out in the open is uncomfortable. I told Al about you, but he refuses to listen."

I feel bad for her, but I have seen Al yell, fight, and even throw people out. The Silver Spoon is a business.

Sometimes when he jokes with me, I don't know if he is serious until he laughs.

I'm afraid of losing my privilege of coming to the strip club like when my hand touches Fire's breasts or buttocks by accident.

"You're naughty." Fire has said when it happened in the past. "You can act innocent to others, but I know the real Steve."

For a moment, I worry, but she smiles and winks at me, reminding me of my female friends, who know me very well. My heart loves Fire. She is my friend. The dances are fun, but I want another date with her.

Fire dances in the corner with me, putting her bosom in my face, but it isn't the same. It is like making love in a living room with people watching us except that the strip club is empty during a Packers game.

"I hate this!" Fire says, kissing my forehead.

I grin. "When can we go out?"

"I have a couple of job interviews and when I land a job, we'll set up a schedule for going out."

I want to believe her, but she always has excuses, like another job interview or her daughter lost gymnastics meet and needed her. I give her the benefit of doubt, but as time passes, I begin to see the truth.

She doesn't answer my calls or emails. I see that it is time to move on.

My mind knows she isn't the right one. I frequent The Silver Spoon less after Fire stood me up again. We had a date to meet at a coffee shop at the mall. I sat in Starbucks for two hours, waiting to feel a tap on my shoulder, hearing her say, "Hello, author." As time ticked by, it dawned on me she wasn't coming.

Dejected, I avoided the club instead drinking at Sal's. When the bus passed The Silver Spoon, I thought of her.

"What am I doing wrong?" I ask Candy visiting the strip club after mustering some guts to return a month later.

Fire hadn't arrived at The Silver Spoon yet. "I had a date with Fire, but she never came. Maybe I should give up on having a girlfriend."

"Any woman would love to have you. Fire is a cocaine addict," Candy says, giving me a sip of beer.

Did she assume I knew? I'm stunned not wanting to believe it at first, but it begins to make sense. I remember seeing her high one night when her grandma died.

She was in a daze, crying and mumbling about her grand-mother until the ladies took her downstairs. Another evening Fire was seen by Al sitting on a man's lap naked and Al pulled her aside. After that she seemed to be on something, I realized Fire had a drug problem. My favorite bus driver, Rich, who worked at The Silver Spoon for five years said, "Steve, Fire has always been an addict." When he picked me up at the club one evening, Rick saw her strung out. My love for Fire didn't disappear.

"I love her."

Candy waits until Al was serving a patron and answered, "I know, Steven."

"She needs help."

"She doesn't want it. All of us have tried. Just leave it. I'm going downstairs to smoke. Candy hugs me before she walks away.

Sitting at the bar I'm confused and hurt not knowing what to think. I sat motionless until I felt a tap on my arm.

"Hi, author. How are you? Fire asks. She takes the envelope from my knee and rips it open to take a twenty out. "Let's do a dance now and one later. Al is in the office. Let's do a private dance in the back."

"Okay." I follow her. I'm nervous about Al seeing us, but Fire isn't worried putting me at ease. I situate the electric wheelchair in the booth.

Naked, Fire splits her legs, placing one on my shoulder, allowing me to see her vagina. She purrs in my ear. Then Fire puts her breasts in my face as the song, "One Moment in Time," plays.

"What's the problem?"

"You."

"Me?"

"You forgot our date at Starbucks a month ago."

"Is that why you haven't been coming around?" Fire sits on the bench and slips her negligee on.

I'm silent. Did Candy tell me the truth? I don't want to believe it. I wrestle with confronting Fire about her drug problem. Is it my business to question what she does with her life?

"I'm sorry. Let's go out this week. I'm free Wednesday afternoon at one. Let's meet at Olive Garden." Fire rubs my knee.

Before I could apply the filter to my mouth, I blurt out, "You're a cocaine addict. Please get some help." My eyes well as I swing my arm to touch her.

She backs away. "Who told you that?" She crosses her arms over her chest.

› WAITING ‹

Time passes as I wait for Fire. The rain drenched her from head to toe. She went directly to the dressing room. We haven't spoken since I accused her of being a coke head.

I have learned to be patient with women. Heather never comes when she says she will. Often, she is an hour or two late.

Kerry, the care manager, complains and then threatened to cancel her services. By this time, I have ejaculated. I still have to pay Heather. It's not worth the money or the hassle. My imagination performs just as well when I'm horny, replaying past sex with Heather.

I smile at Fire.

She opens my apology letter. I used her real name so she understands I'm her friend and not a business transaction. I ask her to meet me at Red Lobster.

Fire puts the letter back in the envelope. "We'll go out when I get a second job. We'll set up a schedule for going out." Fire gives a sip of beer.

I persist. "When are we going out?"

"I'll call you on Monday. I'm applying to the Hilton and the PDQ across the street. My schedule is unpredictable and I don't want to stand you up again."

I want to believe her, but I realize she can also be lying. It's hard for my heart to let go of her. When any woman pays attention to me, I'm in love. I never give up on someone or something I want even when it frustrates me.

In the past people have disappointed or lied to me, causing me to protect myself from getting hurt. I'm careful in believing Fire.

"We'll do lunch or have coffee. Give me time." Fire kisses me on my forehead. "I'll be back."

I nod, turning my attention to the game. The Packers game preoccupies my mind for now. When the Packers are on TV, women are the last thing on my mind. Looking for a girlfriend can wait until the game is over.

Waiting is a part of my life. For two years, I waited to get a communication device working. Four days after my mother passed, I went to the Communication Clinic to meet with my occupational therapist, Holly Atkins. I was half sleep when she greeted me.

"I'm sorry for the loss of your mother. She was a great woman. You'll need a better way to communicate with people now that she's gone. A communication device that scans would be perfect for you. You would sway your head back and forth like you do for Morse code and it's attached to the electric wheelchair. It'll allow you to write, use the Internet, Facebook, read, operate the TV, and talk to people."

We went into the occupational therapy room to trY the communication device. Holly put a tablet on a metal stand in front of me and attached two buddy buttons with Velcro to my head array.

I listened to Holly's instructions and after I tried it, I ordered one.

I was overdue for a new electric wheelchair since my current electric wheelchair was eight years old. Therapists recommend users replace electric wheelchairs every five years. I didn't use my electric wheelchair much when I lived with my mother except when I went out with Bob. I avoided ordering one due to the cumbersome process and logistics involved. Once that's done, it's an endless wait for Medicaid and Medicare to approve it.

I sat with a wheelchair vendor and a physical therapist at a Rehabilitation Center He filled out paperwork, while I listened to him talk about its features. "You should be no problem getting the new wheelchair with your hamstrings, being extra tight, bending your legs ninety degrees."

The older I become the tighter my hamstrings get, curving my legs inward, making it impossible for me to stand.

The wheelchair vendor, Matt, shows me a brochure. "What color do you want?"

Midnight blue reminds me of the strip club. "Blue. When do I get it?"

"Four to six months for approval if we do the paperwork properly and probably two months to order it." Matt wrote a few notes.

I grumbled, knowing through past history it would take a year to receive one.

I went to the Communication Center each Friday for an hour to practice on the communication device while I waited to receive mine.

Most of the time I was tired. I would be up until three in the morning writing or hung over from the strip club. Fire was still on my mind.

The commute to the Communication Center wasted my time. The bus picked up and dropped off people from work. For an hour appointment I rode the bus for a couple of hours both ways. I would rather spend my time writing at home. The day was shot when I returned home to eat supper before taking a nap to work late into night.

"Medicaid won't pay for the Bluetooth for the electric wheelchair to operate the communication device." Holly delivered the grim news to me one day.

"How much is it?"

"Seven hundred dollars. We can appeal it, but it will take a year."

"I have a career and I can't wait anymore. I'm buying it."

Matt ordered the Bluetooth and invoiced my beneficiary agent, April Clark at Wisconsin Special Trust Fund.

Finally, after eight months the new the electric wheelchair arrived. It was incompatible with the communication device. For the next five months Holly tried a mouse control system, but it was too slow and delicate for me to use with my head movement. The head array broke. Plus, the seat of the electric wheelchair didn't fit properly, hurting my butt.

At one session Holly delivered some more news. "I have cancer, but it's treatable. I'm taking off two months."

"I love you. I hope your recovery goes well." I took a deep breath.

I felt enormous gratitude for Holly since she helped me with the Morse code system after my voice recognition software became outdated. Morse code changed my life, enabling me to write with more accuracy. Voice recognition was slow and I had to retrain commands several times to make it work.

I had two books to sell, publicity to write, and another book to compose. My career couldn't be put on hold. I needed access to clear communication.

After Holly returned, she taught me how to read books, use the Internet, access Facebook, communicate with people out in the community, write, email, and text people on the communication device. I made little progress. She wanted me to work on the communication device at home, but I was too busy or lacked an attendant to help me.

The Communication Center required a client to have an attendant with him or her for liability purposes.

Holly couldn't continue to bend the rules. "I can't see you without an attendant."

Paula was elected to accompany me, but moaned about it.

"I can't eat lunch today. I have to drive across town, wasting gas that for which I won't be reimbursed. Just to sit for an hour and you don't even use it."

Paula voiced the same complaint each time we went. I thought about not going to the Communication Center, but I decided I have to keep trying and I needed a new computer.

The Morse code software conflicted with Windows XP and didn't allow the mouse to open web pages on the Internet or use Facebook.

My old computer was also vulnerable to hacking. Next purchase: a new computer.

I renewed my efforts to get the communication device working. Holly saw me bump into walls and doors, knocking the readout on the wheelchair out of place.

"You've no control over your driving and you'll break the communication device. I'm not putting the communication device on the wheelchair until you drive better."

Paula agreed.

I didn't argue. I often bump into things. My heart wasn't into the communication device even though I envisioned working at the strip club on the tablet like everyone else. I could picture myself, emailing my agent or one of my publishers at the strip club while Fire was dancing on the stage. I wanted flexibility to work: downtown, Memorial Union, anywhere.

As I sat on the terrace, I envisioned having a conversation with people or a pretty woman, aided by the communication device.

All of my life, I loved talking with people. Some took the time to understand me, for others, when I was out alone, I needed a device to communicate. Discouraged again, I ignored the communication device and avoided any extra effort to understand it.

Holly emailed me suggesting I spend two hours at the clinic. I didn't want to hear Paula complaining.

I fought an endless battle for my needs. I struggled to get one of my attendants to take me to Walgreens for a flu shot.

When I needed groceries, I waited until my food ran low. Then Kerry or Paula came to me. "We're taking you grocery shopping tomorrow."

With two hundred and twenty-five dollars, I filled my cart. Bread didn't stay fresh that long and would run out first, but I would ask Kerry to get bread once that happened.

When Paula saw my groceries she said, "Your food won't fit in the refrigerator."

I couldn't win. By avoiding arguments, I thought I was making it easier for my attendants. I used a loaner at the Communication Center. My patience in getting the communication device wears thin. It's been months since I ordered the new electric wheelchair and the device.

Paula leaves the occupational therapy room to use the bathroom.

Holly turns to me. "Your staff is here to help you. Please come for two hours a week."

"I can't!" I whisper to Holly. "They're too busy."

"But they're there for you."

So many incidents with my attendants made me tired of the nonsense. My mother had devoted her entire life to me. When I learned a new computer program, she spent countless hours helping me program commands and solving problems. I knew the new communication device would need the same dedication with hours of practice.

Finding the time to practice would be difficult. With some of the staff unable to read, troubleshooting may be an issue.

In the back of my mind I make up excuses as to why I'm not further along.

For all of my life, I talked to people and using a communication device isn't me. The computer voice feels false. At times I do need a communication device, like when I check out a grocery store on my own. People become impatient when they have to ask me to repeat myself several times to understand my words. But the waiting and setbacks dampen my enthusiasm.

My career is finally taking off requiring my time. Now isn't the right time.

Holly confronts Paula when she comes into room. "Would you and the staff have the time to help Steve with the communication device?"

"Absolutely, we always have time for him." Paula sits down.

"He says the staff doesn't have time to help him. Someone needs to mount the device and connect it to the switches in order for him to practice."

"That's a story the author likes to tell so he can write something, making it seem real." Paula stares at me, challenging me to disagree.

I'm quiet, but changes need to happen.

Holly reverts the device back to scan mode since I wasn't making progress with mouse control movements.

I feel defeated and depressed. I truly will never be independent. To have the ability to talk to people out in the community I need someone to attach the buddy buttons to the head array. To leave and travel somewhere else, I need someone to remove the buttons and engage the drive function on the wheelchair.

Then Holly delivers more shocking news. "We've almost used up the funding from Medicaid for getting the communication device to work, and I'm resigning at the end of the month. It's time for a change. I have been an occupational therapist for twenty-five years."

"You'll be put on a waiting list until the Communication Center finds a replacement. Are you willing to come here more often to get that going?"

It's time to go all out.

After the appointment, Paula says, "I'm not coming back to the Communication Center after Holly leaves. You don't try to use it anyway."

Determined to work on the communication device, I return home and spend the rest of the afternoon practicing.

After lunch on Monday, I ask Ajay and Paula, "Please put me in the electric wheelchair to use the communication device."

"I'm going to get my lunch," Paula tells me, holding her car keys in her hand as she begins to walk out of the door.

I despise begging but I am under a deadline.

"Come on, Ajay. Let's get this done so I can get my food." Paula drops her keys on the table, helping Ajay transfer me, putting the buddy buttons on the head array, and turning on the communication device.

"By the way, we're going to the Communication Center on Wednesday and Friday from eleven to two." I give Paula the news while I tap the buttons with my head, using the tablet.

I sit in the living room reading a book on Kindle. Freedom. I'm able to read without attendants turning pages. My Mom turned countless pages. When I moved to the Clove home, I slowly gave up reading when the attendants complained about having to turn pages.

Ralph walks upstairs and asks Ajay, "Where's he going?"

"Nowhere, the author is working," Ajay replies, eating his lunch.

"Oh." Ralph goes back downstairs.

I ignore the interruption and continue to read. If I want to change activities, I still need assistance if I want to write, use Facebook, or use the communication device.

My rear end begins to hurt from sitting in the hard seat of the electric wheelchair.

I make some headway over two afternoons but I also have to check my email and write. A long way to go and a short time to make it happen.

In my writer's mind I believe it's possible to understand the communication device, working hard in the days before Holly leaves. It's like going to an intensified summer school class.

The communication device isn't charged when I visit Holly on Wednesday. We have to wait to use it. I ask questions about how to use Facebook and other technical issues about the tablet.

Holly suggests using a graduate student to show me how to use Facebook and do a search on the Internet.

"I'll ask my writer friends to help me."

Paula is impressed at my interest in the communication device, but then she leaves to answer a call.

I show Holly that I was able to read a book on Kindle, but then something occurs to me. "How do I buy a book on Kindle?"

"I'll set you up with an account." Holly pats me on the shoulder. "And I'll show you how to buy a book."

I watch her set the account up. "I forgot how to open the web page. Can you show me again?"

Paula returns. "I can't come on Friday. Jimmy has a doctor's appointment."

I have already solved the problem. "I'll ask Brian, my counselor to come. I want to be able to write and email. Yesterday I wrote common sentences that I say often to people. Can we put them on communication device then mount the device on the electric wheelchair?"

"I won't be able to do everything before I go. You're going to have to wait. The College of Point has a rehabilitation engineering program and you can apply to Department of Vocational Rehabilitation for financial assistance."

DVR is an employment agency that trains, educates, finds employment, and purchases specialized equipment like computers for people with disabilities. DVR wanted to know if I could even write when I needed a new computer many years ago.

"I'd rather die." I don't hold fond feelings toward DVR, who labeled me as unemployable, which led me to sit at home for two years before going to college.

"DVR will help you with your career," Holly says.

"I'll pay for it."

"We'll talk about it." Holly glances at her wristwatch. "Your bus should be here."

On Friday Brian meets me at the Communication Center and sees the progress that I have made in a week. "You've really worked hard on this."

Holly touches my arm. "I thought that we could attach the head array to the communication device next week. Unfortunately, Matt, the wheelchair vendor broke his foot and won't be working for a month. I leave next Friday. So, it won't be done, but Point can take over."

"I need a new computer, too." I braced myself to hear about DVR. "My computer is XP Windows and it could be hacked. I'll buy a new computer with Windows 10 and have my cousin set it up."

"If you do, it will goof up the settings and you won't be able to write," Holly says. "DVR will help with a computer and the communication device."

"Something to think about." Brian looks at me.

I have reservations about going back to DVR but I want to please Holly and Brian.

"There isn't much that we can do now. This is the last time that we'll get together.

"You're on the right track." Holly begins to cry. "Please go to DVR."

"Thank you for everything, Holly. You've changed my life, making me an author with a career. You're my hero. I love you."

"I have no doubt that you'll make it work and succeed in your endeavors. Your mother is proud of you. And I love you, too." Holly hugs me.

"I'll talk to Eric, your service coordinator about contacting DVR," Brian says.

"Maybe since I'm an author with a literary agent DVR will believe now I can write," I say, looking at Holly and Brian.

I use the communication device that afternoon and a couple of days afterwards, but it takes away time spent emailing or writing.

The communication device sits on the living room table, collecting dust.

Spring turns into summer. A few weeks later, my service coordinator, Eric emails me about DVR. It will take sixty days for DVR to hear my request and they want to know how it will make me employable.

I don't want to argue with them about my writing career or whether I'm employable.

Eric contacted Kate Smart, occupational therapist from College of Point, to set up an appointment.

I didn't wait for a rejection from DVR. My career was taking off. I am doing interviews for the radio and newspapers, book reviews, and book signings. It irks me how small-minded DVR is. It isn't worth my energy when I had demands and problems with my care.

By email, Kate puts together a cost sheet for my services: eighteen dollars for twelve sessions. I sign it immediately.

My staff doesn't know what I have done. Everything I do they must log in my file for the State of Wisconsin: how many bowel movements I have, what I eat, when I sleep, and where I go.

I have complete control over my writing career, which includes hiring an editor. There are limitations with my trust fund like I can't use it to publish or buy copies of books. I'm not allowed to make a profit with my trust money, but I can buy anything without a limitation except for medical equipment restriction. If something can better my life and doesn't cost the total of my trust fund like a house, I can purchase it.

I make decisions involving money such as spending two hundred dollars for a cab in order to attend a friend's wedding. It scares me at times to spend my money. I want to save it, watching it grow in my checking account or my trust fund. I'm aware of the amount in my trust not spending much of it, saving a large sum for my future. Money enables me to buy a computer or a shower chair when I need it. It brings me happiness seeing friends, going places, creating career opportunities, and meeting new people. I'm a cheapskate, being careful with my money.

Time doesn't stop, however, for an up-and-coming author. I keep writing and promoting my books, but the mouse doesn't open the web pages off the Internet.

How can I be an author without the ability to Google? Another expenditure I must make.

One night while I'm at the strip club, Fire says, "Have your staff set up a Facebook page for you and we can chat anytime."

It frustrates me that I only communicate with Fire in person. People take for granted the ability to dial a phone and talk. I'm excited about the idea and schedule time with Kate.

My first appointment with Kate, she comes to Clove house. I sign more paperwork. With the buddy buttons on the head array, I show Kate how I use Kindle, the Internet, and my vocabulary common sentences to communicate with people from my office.

She watches me work the communication device, taking notes on a steno pad.

I tap away at the buddy buttons, working hard so she sees my determination.

Kate sits in silence for a long time. "That's good. I want to see you do Morse code at your computer."

Ajay and Paula transfer me to the manual wheelchair. I tap Morse code and send Kate an email.

We break as I drink water and use the bathroom.

"Now show me how you use Word."

She jots her notes, making me wonder what her recommendation will be as I enter the sentence in the Word document.

"Can I make it work?" I'm anxious to hear Kate's idea.

"I'm one hundred percent positive that you can use it, using Morse code." Kate smiles at me. "You're more efficient at Morse code than at scanning. And I'm absolutely sure that we can attach the communication device to the electric wheelchair. With some research I believe that I'll be able to interface the communication device and the computer with Morse code."

I envision writing a novel at the Memorial Union or communicating with the farmers' market vendor.

"When I get back from my vacation, I'll write my evaluation and send it to you. After I contact Matt, the wheelchair representative, and the communication device manufacturer, we'll get you going. Does that sound like a plan?"

I imagine Googling dating websites, finding a girlfriend.

I feel great about how the day went. I'm finally getting somewhere. I expect slow progress as they integrate my communication device. Until then I will pursue more publicly and start writing another manuscript.

What if it doesn't work, what then? My apprehension is real. Using XP is a risk–my computer could be hacked. Then what will I do? It's my lifeline to the outside world. It's how I resolve problems and issues.

I email Matt in the early morning about the wheelchair.

When I get up later, Ajay says, "The wheelchair guy will be here at one."

I smile, feeling a great sense of independence.

My cousin, Larry is still adjusting to me being independent. He worries I will use up my trust fund money and wants me to save it. He emails me about free computer, two years old with Windows. I nix his idea to save me money with a used computer that I will have to replace in a year or two. Integrating my devices with a computer is a bigger investment of money, time, and energy. My trust is there to improve my life, to buy computers, go on vacations, and pay veterinarian bills. When I die, the State receives the money in my trust and I want to use most of the fund instead of the government getting it.

A brand-new computer will ensure Morse code and Co-Writer (the word prediction software) will work. Then I'm stuck. I continue to write, email, and wait. I email Kate.

Labor Day comes and goes without an evaluation from Kate. I wait another two weeks and send another email. My parents can't help me. Ralph's mother and father always are there for him with each decision. It is up to me to find out what is going on.

I wait for her reply. Time moves on as pages of a novel are written. I can't get mad or quit, but my career is at risk without a new computer.

Finally, Kate replies that she is working with Matt to resolve some issues. The applications I want uploaded on the computer and the tablet complicate integration. It will cost one thousand dollars to purchase a new computer and a printer. Matt requires an additional fifteen-hundred dollars to synchronize the communication device with the electric wheelchair and sixteen-hundred dollars for the output box and the head array for my old electric wheelchair as a backup.

I don't hesitate. I'm spending about five-thousand dollars on technology that will hopefully change my life, but there are no guarantees. I'm making adult decisions.

I'm working in my office the next afternoon when Jerry comes to see me. "Why aren't you using the communication device?"

I open my mouth to answer, but Paula interrupts. "He doesn't use it now that Holly has resigned. That lady, who was here for one day and worked with Steve, didn't come back."

I laugh.

Jerry grumbles. "What's so funny?"

"I'm working on it, just like writing a new book or women." My life is under my control. I burst into laughter. Sometimes it is easier for me to laugh than get mad at people.

It angers me when my staff doesn't allow me to answer for myself as if I'm incapable. I shrug off Paula's interruption instead and avoid an argument with Paula that would lead me nowhere.

Laughter helps me to forget the pain of waiting.

THE PAINTER, RACHEL

I keep waiting for a girlfriend when a woman unexpectedly enters into my life.

I'm writing away in the living room when a case manager, Tina from Integration Residential, taps me on my shoulder, making me jump.

"I didn't mean to scare you. We know a woman with Cerebral palsy, who paints with her head. Her name is Rachel Bond. I thought that the two of you would like to get together. Here's her email address."

My eyes light up as I read the email address on the Post-it note. After Tina leaves, I tap my message to Rachel introducing myself and asking her if she would like to meet.

When Rachel responds several days later, she invites me to her apartment. I daydream about our meeting. "Kerry, order the bus. Rachel wants to see me." I smile.

Kerry comes into my room. "What's the ruckus?"

"I have got a date in two days."

While riding the bus to see Rachel, I wonder what she's like or if she's cute. My mind races. Will she like me? What will we talk about? I'm excited and nervous at the same time.

The bus driver, Mark, pulls into a parking lot of an apartment building. My wide grin is plastered on my face.

"You can't get enough of women," Mark says, operating the lift. "I'll get the front door."

I make my way up the sidewalk and then negotiate a long winding ramp. Mark holds open the outside and the inside door. "Have fun, player."

I navigate through the lobby up another ramp and down a halfway. At the end of the corridor, I knock on the door with my left foot for several minutes. I almost give up. A male care attendant opens the door. "I'm Franklin. Rachel is waiting for you."

I drive into the apartment. Rachel is painting with a brush attached to a head stick.

Rachel smiles and nods at me as paint drips from the brush onto her smock.

"I'm Steve. How are you?"

Rachel's fine black hair flows across her shoulders. Her blue eyes acknowledge me as she nods.

Franklin removes her paintbrush and takes Rachel to the bathroom to clean her off.

I admire her canvas, the picturesque rainbow with a blue sky over the turquoise ocean as dolphins leap out of the water. Different colors of paint clutter the wooden easel bench, reminding me of my desk when I'm rewriting a manuscript.

I like Rachel already. She crafts something from her imagination.

It's refreshing to see a person with the same dedication and passion that I have for a creative career. I appreciate the painting's blend of color, skill, and her effort with each brushstroke it takes to create the picture.

Her paintings hang around the beautiful apartment. I surmise every picture has a meaning behind it just like each book shares a message. The brilliant array of colors sends me into a daydream.

"What are you thinking?" Rachel asks. She smiles at me.

I shake myself from my reverie. "I'm admiring your artwork. It is awesome. You're talented."

Rachel uses her eyes, staring at her tablet, picking out common sentences and characters, spelling out slowly creating words, leading to phrases. Her communication device speaks for her. "Thank you. I hear you're quite the author."

"I just write books."

She laughs and then composes a new message. "That isn't what Jerry told me.

Let's go to the rooftop and talk."

I follow Rachel. Franklin rides up the elevator with us. He holds open doors and lets us out on the walkway. "I'll be inside when you want to go back downstairs."

The view is breathtaking with treetops in all directions and off in the distance, the grey cupola of the Capitol towers. The cloudless blue sky reminds me of my mother in heaven.

Rachel asks, "What are you thinking about?"

"My Mom. It has been a year without her. Life is so different and new. I can do what I want. It is hard making decisions. Sometimes I want to be with Mom, but I keep going."

"I'm sorry."

"It's a new life. I'm on my own now. It's just me and my cat, Lindy. In one night, I entered adulthood, making decisions right and left. It doesn't stop. I guess that's life."

Rachel doesn't respond. No one does in these situations.

I search the sky for the meaning of life. "Where are your parents?"

"My parents are divorced. Mom lives in Green Bay and Dad lives nearby. I see them all of the time. They take me places, like the Wisconsin Dells. Do you travel?"

I'm envious. "I went to Lambeau Field each fall to see the Packers with my cousin."

Now I can't travel without a care attendant. It upsets me that my staff gets to on vacations, but I'm not allowed a trip because they refuse to travel with me.

I want to be sarcastic, but I hold my tongue. I change the subject. "Do you have siblings?"

"No," Rachel answers. "What about you?"

"I have a sister and two nieces in Milwaukee. My sister works sixty hours a week as a computer technician and is a single parent. I rarely see her, but I understand." I yawn. "I work too much, too."

"I can relate to that. Painting takes all of my energy, but I love it." Rachel smiles at me.

"Your artwork is gorgeous. You're talented and cute." I'm falling in love with her already.

Rachel blushes. "You're handsome and sweet."

The compliment goes straight to my head. I laugh imagining her being my girlfriend. My mind flips to us having sex. I can't help it. I'm a man, and want the physical passion of a woman. It must be written on my face.

Rachel sticks out her tongue. "That's all men think about."

I try to be coy.

"Don't play dumb with me. S-e-x."

I laugh at Rachel's answer. "Why do women know everything?"

"Because we do. Men are predictable, especially you." Rachel taps me on my shoulder with her hand.

"What do you like to do other than painting?"

"I enjoy reading and writing. And what do you like other than women?" Rachel laughs.

"Football and basketball."

She uses her eyes to spell or predict words with her communication device.

"Typical male. I have a boyfriend, Jacob. He is a big sports fan. Jacob lives in Black Falls and we visit each other."

My heart sinks but that doesn't stop me. I think that I can win her over with my irresistible charm and Jacob isn't nearby.

A couple of minutes later, Franklin comes. "Excuse me it's time for his bus."

We continue to see each other off and on during the summer, visiting many places together.

I tell Rachel everything. She relates to how my life is. One time, we are driving our wheelchairs along a bike trail at a park near her apartment when a person approaches us and asks, "Are you two all right alone. Should I get help?"

It frustrates us when strangers think we are useless, stupid, or dumb. Some mean well, but still! Even though it unnerves us, we laugh to suppress our anger.

Rachel and I have successful careers yet people assume we are cognitively disabled. Both of us have been on the local TV and newspaper articles, showing our achievements. We are blazing a trail for others to follow in our footsteps in the future.

Rachel and I sit next to a pavilion where magnificent oaks and maples along the park's borders sway in the light breeze. The scent of the wildflowers drifts by. The city skyline rises in the distance. Puffy cottonwood balls float through the air. The two of us enjoy the quiet solitude.

We fall asleep in the peaceful silence. I relax in my light slumber.

After a while I say, "It is quiet here. No cell phones, no TVs or radios, no yelling, and arguing. I don't sleep well at home. All that they do is bicker and make noise, waking me up."

Rachel nods and smiles at me.

"They think that they can watch TV in the living

room when I want to watch a game and they watch garbage. I pay rent. They work for me. I live and work there."

"Staff think they can take their sweet time after I call them. They're always on the phone. Talking about what, I don't have a clue. And it is always important." I wait for Rachel's to compose her response.

"Yes, I know. A good night's sleep is impossible because they're cleaning at night or talking on the phone. I don't sleep either. My muscles wake me up." Rachel lives in a two-bedroom apartment with her roommate, Robert, and a twenty-four-seven staff.

I tell her. "My left arm flies up and I can't relax it without great effort. It keeps me awake. My room is so hot that I sleep naked without a sheet on." She would fulfill my desire if she was there, naked, beside me at night.

"That's a man for you," Rachel says, laughing uncontrollably.

Would she sleep naked? I don't ask. I'm a gentleman. My favorite fantasy is being in the shower and having an attendant ask, "Steve can April, (I named my fantasy woman) join you?"

I replace April with a naked nonverbal woman and it becomes more meaningful.

We would stare at each other while warm water cascades over us, relaxing our tense muscles. Then we touch each other's genitals with our hands. My semen flows onto her fingers as I rub her between her legs. She puts my semen inside of her.

The fantasy is my dream that I replay in my mind

thousands of times and when next to Rachel it intensifies. I'm falling in love with her.

Being with Rachel makes me happy, dancing during an outdoor concert, listening to classical music at The Concert on the Square, or sitting side by side enjoying a beautiful summer's night.

I want people to believe that Rachel is my girlfriend. I want to believe that Rachel is my girlfriend.

Then she pounds in reality when she says, "Jacob doesn't mind that I see you. He understands. I don't get jealous when he goes out with women friends."

I didn't want to hear that. I love Rachel. We do things together as if we are boyfriend and girlfriend. She tells me she is in love with Jacob, but he lives up north and it's not easy to see him to see her.

"How did you meet Jacob?"

"We dated in college. He was able-bodied when we met, but a car accident paralyzed him. Through the years we remained friends and eventually fell in love. Jacob's brother drives him to visit me or my Dad takes me to Black River to see him."

"What does he do?" I want to know if I stand a chance against Jacob.

"He's a CPA."

I don't know what to say. He's well educated like me. My spirit breaks and my mind rebels. I want Rachel for myself.

My heart chooses to ignore those four words: "I have a boyfriend."

When I'm with Rachel, it feels like we are a couple, spending time together attending different events. She gives me happiness in the new strange life I'm still adjusting to. I'm grateful that she is a part of my life now. Rachel helps me look beyond my petty problems at home.

Rachel treats me to the movies. I don't like the cinema, but I enjoy sitting next to her, being with her, and hearing her laugh. One time we are watching a movie and she leaves during an explicit sex scene. I am uncomfortable but also engrossed seeing a couple on screen making love. I don't notice her leave. I look over and I'm alone.

What is wrong, I wonder? I watch the rest of the movie to avoid disrupting the theater, hoping that she is okay. When I come out of the movie, Rachel is waiting for me in the lobby with a smile on her face.

I drive my wheelchair over to her.

"Did I do something wrong?"

"I'll tell you later at home. Let's go." Rachel exits the front door.

I follow her out and down a couple of blocks to her apartment. We laugh and knock our electric wheelchairs like bumper cars along the sidewalk. Inside her apartment, Rachel invites me into her bedroom. I park the wheelchair in her room.

"Franklin, please turn on my radio and close the door. Thank you." Rachel waits for Franklin to leave.

I listen to soft rock, enjoying the moment.

For several minutes her silence muffles the music. She seems conflicted until finally her device delivers her shocking message: "I don't like sex because I was raped by a care attendant. That's why I left the movie. I'm sorry."

"I'm so sorry." I hadn't thought about sex as harmful. I feel guilty. I would never want to hurt Rachel and I decide to stop talking about sex to her even though I think about it all of the time.

The awkward silence intensifies. I nervously look around her room, searching for another topic to discuss. The constant beep of Rachel's feeding machine provides an underlying beat to the music. "Do you miss eating?"

"I do. A year ago, food lodged in my lungs, making me choke. I wasn't able to fully clear the food causing pneumonia. The doctors inserted a feeding tube in my belly. I especially miss chocolate. When I visit my Mom, we cheat by having chocolate ice cream."

I am lucky to be able to eat solid foods. I admire Rachel's strength.

"It's suddenly giving up something that you love and adjusting to something totally new," she says.

"It is like my Mom. Clove house doesn't feel like home. When I enter that house at night, it feels like visiting a stranger. And being told no one cares about me or I don't care about people. It makes me want to die. I think about killing myself."

Tears spill from Rachel's eyes, making it difficult to use her communication device. After several minutes, Rachel speaks. "Please don't. A few of my disabled friends committed suicide, taking a small piece of my heart with them. I couldn't take another suicide. I have horrible thoughts sometimes, too. Please don't make me go through that again. I'm always here if you ever need someone to talk to."

"I promise." I find warmth in the eyes.

The more time I spend with Rachel, the more I love and admire her as a person. Of course, I fall in love with her, hoping that Jacob disappears from her life, making me her boyfriend.

We explore the Art Fair on the Square one afternoon. We browse the tents, looking at the different types of artwork, admiring the beautiful pieces. I hurry past the tent, emanating with the scent of baked cinnamon rolls even though my mouth is watering.

When we come across a vendor with watercolor paintings, Rachel spends extra time there, examining the colors and the textures before introducing herself to the painter. "Hi, I'm Rachel Bond. I like your work and I paint watercolors, too."

She talks to painters like I do with writers and authors. It amazes me how the cerebral palsy vanishes out of me when I'm with writers. The recognition is something that I treasure and I know that Rachel does, too.

This bond, linking two people by a profession or love is what I enjoy. It reminds that I'm not alone in the world. Being with Rachel is special to me.

My mind wants more. When I email Rachel asking to go out, she is sick, going away, or her electric wheelchair is broken. It saddens me when Rachel isn't available to go out. I crave female attention. When I need a woman, I visit Fire at the strip club.

A stripper, Star, resembles Rachel in skin tone and has short brown hair. I laugh when Star is called on the stage, I imagine Rachel Bond.

My mind delves into the dirty recesses of my desires. I can't help it. I can't make up my mind if I want an able-bodied or disabled woman for a girlfriend.

With a non-disabled woman, I can easily go out to eat or have a drink with her. Fantasies like traveling, staying at a hotel, and making love to a woman in a hotel room play in my mind.

I want a woman to hold me when nothing is going right and tell me that tomorrow is a new day. When I sit at a bar, I imagine sitting with a woman, teasing her as she holds my hand. I want to kiss her under the stars with her body pressing against mine.

When my mother passed, I lost my confidant. She left a gaping black hole in my heart. My mother loved me unconditionally and completely. As time ticks on, I realize no woman can fill it, but Rachel comes close.

I discuss financial purchases, bounce ideas off of her, and voice complaints. "I have to buy Bluetooth for the communication device because Medicare won't pay for it," or "I peed in my pants on purpose when the overnight attendant left in the middle night and Kerry discovered me, sitting at the computer wet when she arrived for the a.m. shift. Kerry called Jerry to fire the attendant after I told them that the attendant needed to go a week earlier."

When I tell Rachel the story she nods and laughs. "I have been there."

At the county fair Rachel kicks her feet and thrashes her arms, listening to "Take This Job and Shove It," I sing the lyrics, wishing all of my problems would disappear. Whenever I'm with Rachel, the problems fade for a while.

We drive our electric wheelchairs through the livestock barns. The horses prance around a ring. Then we look at the swine, and the cows. It feels like that we are a couple.

People smile at us.

"The player has a girlfriend," says the bus driver when he takes her off the bus.

Maybe the bus driver's comment prompted her to write. She reminds me in an email that I'm a fine catch, but she's in love with Jacob. She has faith I'll find my special someone. I just need to be patient.

I love Rachel. My mind knows that she is taken, but I want a girlfriend. The word "girlfriend" echoes in my soul, driving me crazy at times. My female friends try to console me. "Be patient. It will happen."

I dive into my writing, forgetting about Rachel and women for a while. Writing and football allow me to disappear to another world. Once football season starts, women take a back seat.

The seasons change and I see Rachel less. Cold, snow, wind, and ice don't work well with electric wheelchairs. Sometimes I visit or meet Rachel for a movie. When I see her, it feels like I'm her boyfriend.

Once the frigid temperatures of December hit, I stop seeing Rachel altogether. I shop at the grocery store once a month. Once a week I visit the strip club to see Fire and Sal's to watch the Packers with the guys. Life is good, but when I write my Christmas letter to my family and friends, I make a big mistake.

I mention that I'm in love with Rachel.

My friend Bob addresses the envelopes and sends out my Christmas cards. I put a letter in Rachel's Christmas card. I don't think much about it, believing that Rachel loves me too.

In my heart Rachel is my girlfriend but, in my mind, I know she isn't. When I hear the word girlfriend, it pops into my head and it distorts my thinking. I want my family and friends to be happy for me.

A few days later I receive a blistering email from Rachel. She didn't appreciate me advertising my sentiments toward her to my friends. She already has a boyfriend, Jacob. She reminds me of my position as her friend, not boyfriend.

I sit at the computer for several minutes, feeling bad about hurting Rachel. I take a few minutes to consider my reply. I apologize and hope that my error in judgment didn't jeopardize our friendship.

On New Year's Eve, I take the bus to Sal's to watch college football bowl games, but the bar is hosting a private party so it's closed. I go down State Street, looking for a bar on a frigid night.

Ben, the bus driver, stops me. "I can't let you be out here alone. Get on the bus and I'll take you home."

"I'm not going home. I want to celebrate. Clove house is depressing as hell." Jimmy is probably already sound asleep.

Ben, a good friend, knows I don't like being home. "Wait there." He hops in the bus.

He returns saying, "The dispatcher says you can ride with me until midnight."

I get on the ramp.

Ben makes pickups and drop-offs around Madison while I look at the Christmas lights. A bitter cold wind blows making the snow drift in places. It is tranquil and peaceful, but the dark makes me feel lonely.

"A penny for your thoughts." Ben drives past Rachel's apartment building.

Silence for a minute, I watch the snowflakes fly in the air before I respond. "Life, I guess. Being alone sucks. I want sex, but I want more than that. My dream is to have a companion to share with my life with. I work so hard and make decisions every day. I'm tired. I fear being all alone."

"I know what you mean." Ben looks at me through the overhead mirror. "All of us have the same kind of fear."

The wind howls, surrounding the bus, creeping inside. The coming year I will release two books within a month. A star twinkles in the sky, giving me hope for the future. I know more work is ahead of me with publicity to sell those books, shifting to the role of businessman. Deep inside my heart aches and selling books offers a poor consolation.

Time marches on. I keep writing while the snow flies outside of my office window. Work doesn't end just like the snow never seems to stop. When I'm not at the computer, I think about sex.

I arrange to meet Heather. It's a bold move but I email Rachel requesting advice on how she and Jacob have intercourse. My legs are bent because of my tight hamstrings. I preface my response by alluding that I met someone.

A few days go by without a reply from Rachel, making me worry that I have offended her. She finally answers one evening. She is happy for me and asks about Heather, whether she's disabled or able-bodied. She reveals that she and Jacob lay on their sides when they do it. She assures me everything fits together. Then she suggests meeting to see a movie.

I feel guilty about lying to Rachel, but I want to know if it's possible whether disabled couples can engage in intercourse.

Rachel and I eventually meet up for a movie. She waits in the theater's lobby with a big smile on her face. "Where is she?"

"Who?"

"Your girlfriend. That's who! I hoped to meet her." Rachel looks all around for a woman.

I don't understand who Rachel is talking about, but then it dawns on me, she means Heather. "Heather is a hooker."

I look at Rachel to see what her reaction about

Heather, but she just nods seeming to understand. "I couldn't wait anymore. The deed is done. It was fun. I'm working on my stripper for a second date and I'm not having much luck."

"Be patient. It will happen."

"I'm sorry about wanting to be your boyfriend, but I love you as a friend." I wait for her reaction.

"I love you, too. We're friends."

> THE BUS <

I'm sitting with my disabled peers in a large conference room at the city library for a public hearing about the bus system. I decide to go to find out what is about.

When I see TV cameras and disabled people crying, I realize I have a story to write. An author is always on the hunt for new material.

A spokeswoman stands in front of the conference room, tapping the microphone which doesn't work. The audience grumbles because they can't hear her. The agitation of the crowd rises.

I say to myself, "You have one hundred disabled people here and you don't have a decent mike."

After replacing the microphone, the woman says, "Testing, one, two, three. Can you hear me now?"

A resounding "yes" comes from the audience.

"I'm Crystal Clark from Metro Mobility. Metro Mobility will be ending door-to-door bus service, beginning February. Passengers who receive curb service will pay four dollars a ride, starting January first. We know that these changes are painful to our passengers. We have no choice due to budget cuts."

"The city council is voting on this important matter in a few weeks and we want to get your opinions on the issue. Your name will be called and you'll have five minutes to state your case to the panel of alders represented here the in front. This should give everyone a chance to be heard. Thank you."

For two and a half hours, I listen to passionate pleas from disabled citizens.

"I can't sit out in the cold. I get frostbite easily."

"I can't afford to pay the four dollars bus fare on my fixed income."

"Some disabled people can't handle money and the physically disabled can't hand money to the bus driver."

"People come all over the country to see how our specialized transportation works for their communities and we are going back to the dark ages where the disabled are shut-ins!"

"The employment rate for the disabled is ninety percent compared to eight percent is the rest of the nation. People will lose their jobs because of these changes."

I take it all in. I notice the disabled are not yelling at the alders and the sentiments are heartfelt and realistic. I don't talk, but I move the electric wheelchair to the front as people leave to show my face without saying anything. I'm angry, but I'm already thinking what my next move will be.

At home as Kerry helps me with the urinal, I discuss

the proposed changes with her. "We will have to pay four dollars for a ride, starting in February if the city council passes it and sit out by the curb."

Jimmy calls, needing something from Kerry.

"Tell Jimmy about the bus."

Kerry walks to Jimmy's bedroom. Jimmy, loudly but clearly, bellows, "I can't afford four dollars a ride. I won't go to Catholic Charities anymore. I'll just stay home."

Jimmy used to go to Catholic Charities every Monday and Thursday from nine to one. Lately he attends Catholic Charities twice a month. The other places he goes to is the grocery store once a month and of course his many doctor's appointments.

He sleeps more now.

I yawn, waiting for Kerry to give me some water. I spend the early hours of the morning writing my newest novel. My mind focuses on developing characters.

Later as I process the proposed changes, it upsets me. I probably won't go out as much. It's mid-December and winter is here. Temperatures dip into the twenties at night.

I need time to determine what the new changes to the bus mean to me and people like Ralph. But first I critique student papers, then a college student is interviewing me for the college newspaper.

The electric wheelchair is broken again.

The more I ponder the bus changes. I realize I need to stir up public opinion.

I also need keep my name out there in order to sell

books. After thinking, I email freelance writers Allen and Joe. They write articles for local newspapers and have connections to the TV news stations.

With my expertise as an author, I suggest writing an editorial about the proposed changes to Metro Mobility from the perspective of a user on the importance of specialized transportation for people with disabilities.

Allen responds the next day, advising me to contact Ned Manel, from *News Nine* for the editorial.

Joe replies that he will contact his editor at The Progressive.

My creative juices flow. I write a one-hundred-word editorial in four hours. Short, sweet, and to the point. After some editing and tweaking, I ask Kerry to read it. She nods, clearly impressed.

"I did it again. I'm the awesome author." I laugh.

"No, I'm awesome to put up with you." Kerry makes a goofy face.

After my nap, I email the editor, Ned at *News Nine*, introducing myself. I attach my letter, extolling the vital service Metro Mobility transit provides:

The Expensive Bus Rides:

Imagine having to sit out in a wheelchair in the cold, snow, wind, and the rain, waiting for twenty minutes to take a Para transit bus to work each day. Then picture paying $4 for a bus ride and having only $300 spending money a month. The city council tries to hide the major change, affecting hundreds of disabled Dane County citizens.

Ninety percent of people with disabilities in Dane County are unemployed compared to 8% of the state. The disabled make less than the minimum wage. People with disabilities can only earn $900 a year in order to remain eligible to receive Medicaid and Medicare to pay for our care.

How can the disabled afford to live on a fixed income and pay for bus rides? A majority of the disabled are cognitively handicapped, unable to handle money or wait outside. Having a job gives the disabled person self-confidence. People with disabilities look forward to going to work. I can't live without the bus. Now I can't afford the bus.

Ned Manel responds the next afternoon and agrees to read it on all of the newscasts that day.

"Hey, hey, hey. I'm on TV," I yell. "Come here now." I want a pat on the back and an "attaboy Steve!"

Kerry walks into the office. "What is it?"

The excitement in my voice slurs my speech. "I'm on TV. Get nine now, please."

Kerry changes the channel.

Ned introduces my letter to the editor. "Steven Salmon, an author with severe Cerebral Palsy writes..."

I listen to my words come to life, hopefully, making a small difference in the world. I'm a real author. I'm a real person.

Ralph in the next room says to Teresa, "What's Steve yelling about now? He's bad."

It bothers me that Ralph thinks that I'm a bad person, but after I have yelled at him a couple of times, he's afraid of me. I know that's my fault. Changing his mind is impossible.

Ned finishes reading my letter.

I'm proud. "The author strikes again. I win."

"You're crazy," Kerry tells me.

"I'm the author and you're psycho." I laugh.

Ralph yells louder to Teresa. "Steve needs to behave. He's being mean to Kerry. I don't like him. He's evil."

I know I'm one of the good guys.

The next day The Progressive's editor, Gene Donaldson, emails me.

One of his reporters will be contacting me to interview me for an article in the next issue.

My work makes people stop and think about the consequences to the disabled.

It is not easy to get bus tickets anymore. I can't email Jerry, the Integration Residential Services director, to order more bus tickets. Metro Mobility now prohibits care agencies from purchasing tickets for their clients. My service coordinator, Peter Waters at the Alliance of Living, can order bus tickets. When I request tickets', it turns out the Alliance of Living had already processed the bus tickets for the month.

I would have to wait and conserve my twenty bus tickets until I receive my next allotment of tickets in two months. I email four people requesting information on how to buy additional bus tickets. Peter replies that I can purchase bus tickets in person at the Metro Mobility office and Alliance will reimburse me. I have two tickets left. I forward the email to Kerry, who is home, asking her to buy more bus tickets.

My life consists of playing email tag with people, finding the right person to answer a specific question or perform a specific task. It's the hardest part of being on my own and being disabled. If I don't do it, the issue doesn't go away. I'm an adult now. It exhausts me at times.

I solve my problems. I find answers to my questions. I can accomplish anything by being persistent.

Sometimes I resign that my only choice is to stop going out. Ralph works or plays basketball each day.

When Jimmy goes out, I stop playing the martyr and start scheduling bus rides again.

I go to Sal's to watch the Packers games with the guys and the playwrights' group.

The disabled are the first ones sacrificed and I'm sick of it. People want tax cuts to buy gadgets and fast food that they don't need, but can cut programs for people with disabilities who have real needs.

Most people can't imagine spending only three hundred for essentials. Seventy-five goes to buy household supplies. Two hundred and twenty-five dollars a month for food. Receiving only three hundred dollars a month to spend on other things I want, doesn't cover much.

My food budget is tight. This includes cat food, cat litter, and baby wipes. I go through two boxes of cleansing wipes each month, costing me thirty dollars. I buy toilet paper with my food budget even though I don't use it, but I'm required to contribute to the household.

My agency makes up rules on what residents have to purchase with our food budget. Plastic bags, used to separate pieces of meat when the case manager receives the seventy-five dollars from the food budget to purchase household supplies.

I'm frugal with my spending money, limiting my food purchases to items on sale. Some of my free money goes to buy more food like fresh vegetables, fruits and homemade jam. That's what I want. It is more expensive, but it is healthier than processed foods and taste better.

I spurge occasionally on female entertainment, but I can go without it. I reserve some of my spending money for emergencies like the computer. It doesn't seem right to me to ask the disabled to use half of their spending money on transportation.

People will see someone like me, sitting in the snow, waiting for the bus, and call the police. They'll think we're lost or confused. Once that happens a few times and word get to the mayor, curb service will get kicked to the curb. Hopefully.

I think about suicide. I picture myself at the pier behind the Memorial Union, sitting in the dark on a warm autumn night. I park on the edge of the pier, take my seat belt off and fall into the water. My electric wheelchair sits there as a reminder of my life. Will people miss me? Will they be sad? Will the disabled community ask who will publicize our social issues?

Suicide isn't an option for me. I overcame too much. But having to fight every time and seeing my independence stripped away takes a toll. I must advocate against the proposed changes to Metro Mobility. I need to do more.

In my imagination, I have power, I am an activist. I will make an impact on city hall.

I trudge on a snowy evening to witness the council vote on the bus changes. A puffy powder covers me, including my hair, as I wait outside the glass double doors. I'm freezing and the stiff wind takes my breath away. I continue to wait hoping that someone will open the door for me before the wires short-circuit and render my electric wheelchair inoperable.

A kind woman opens the double glass doors. I follow the signs to the council chambers, leaving a pair of dirty wet tread marks on the white linoleum. The heat warms my icy hands. I park in the empty room with the alders and the mayor, who ready themselves to vote on the bus changes. A pool of water forms underneath my wheelchair, staining the red carpet. Drool drips onto my Packer parka.

The mayor speaks. "The council will now vote on the new changes to Metro Mobility. We need passengers to pay four dollars a ride and we are recommending door-to-door service to be replaced by curb service. Does anyone object to the changes?"

I glare at the council, silent in my fury.

The mayor sees me. "How can I help you?"

In a fit of anger, I fling my arm freeing the envelope taped my left knee. The envelope flies in the air, landing in front of the mayor. "Open it."

"I know who you are. You're the author." The mayor opens the letter and reads it.

At the end of the letter I ask for someone to open the door for me.

The alders and the mayor would give me a round of applause and the mayor would walk me out.

"Where's your attendant?" he might ask. The snow falls in big heavy flakes.

"They're not allowed to accompany me when I leave my home. My staff can only help me inside of Clove house. Something about liability. It's more rules. I'm my own guardian. I go where I want and I do what I want."

The mayor opens the door. "We'll think about what you said and take it into account in our decision."

I venture out in the snow and the suffocating cold wind. The snow blinds me as I slowly drive to the bus. My tight muscles make it difficult for me to drive the electric wheelchair.

Fighting city hall in my mind yields no results. The proposed bus changes pass by a narrow margin.

I go to Sal's to sulk, watch football, and drink with

the guys. My new electric wheelchair sits in the living room, waiting for Sundays to come.

When the football season ends, I quit going out. I still dream of writing the great American novel, I watch basketball, and try to sleep. Kerry shops for my groceries.

The bus changes go into effect. Ralph complains to Paula about them.

"My Mom says that I can't go to work or the gym anymore because of the bus. Why?"

I feel sorry for Ralph. He doesn't understand why something he loves to do is being taken away. Budget cuts, stupid rules, and bureaucratic paperwork are part of our lives. It makes me mad. I understand the impact tax cuts have on the disabled.

Another obstacle or roadblock stymies my path forward until I find a way around it.

Ralph continues his rant to Paula. "I hate the bus. The bus doesn't care about me. I'm going downstairs to watch TV." Ralph slams the basement door.

Two months after the bus changes took effect, I have rarely left Clove house. My roommate, Jimmy, goes twice a month to Catholic Charities and Ralph doesn't talk to anyone after his parents couldn't afford bus fare.

Ralph sits in the living room, watching old reruns and talking to his parents on the phone in the early morning hours, waking me up. His telephone conversation grates on my nerves. He talks about mundane, trivial things. He reports on his menu for the day, TV shows he'll watch, followed by bashing me for being evil to him. Then he'll promise he'll to be nice to me.

I hide in my office and bedroom, avoiding Ralph as much as possible. The isolation makes me feel like I'm suffocating or drowning under water. In my subconscious it is as if I'm dying. The world beckons me to explore it, but after a year of experiencing what the world has to offer, bus cuts have taken it away.

It reminds me of Ralph, whose doctor put him on a balanced diet after a significant weight gain. He remembers the sweets, knows they're bad, but wants them anyway.

I can go out, but I go cold turkey instead of choosing wisely how many times I leave Clove house. My problem is that once I begin to go out, I won't want to stop going places. It is like women or sex. I want more, but I deny myself the pleasure in order to have some money in my checking account. Who can practice moderation when temptation is strong?

› LIFE ‹

A new care attendant, Mike, reads a letter. "A new adult day-care center is opening on Aberg Avenue. Jimmy and Steve should check it out. They're always home."

I'm eating supper at the dining room table. I'm puzzled by Mike's comment.

Today I worked with my literary agent and my middle grade book publisher. "I work every day and have a career. What would I do at adult day-care? Nothing. I would be bored. I do go out."

"You mean that you used to. You haven't been anywhere for a month."

"I go out when I want." I hit Mike in the stomach with my left hand.

"That's not nice." Ralph wiggles his finger at me. "You need to apologize."

"You can't tell me what to do, stupid!" I shoot back.

"Paula, he called me a bad name. Make him apologize."

"Shut up." I fire the "F" word at Ralph several times. "Go to hell, retard."

Mike stands up. "You know that you're wrong saying that word. Apologize."

"That's enough." Paula moves my manual wheelchair away from Ralph.

"Paula, he's being mean. I want an apology from him." Ralph hides behind Mike. He looks afraid.

"Fuck you." I lose control. I know I'm wrong. The frustration from my self-imposed confinement and isolation boils over.

"Stop it. We're a family." Paula tries to diffuse the confrontation. She puts both hands up in front of me as if to halt my verbal attacks.

"We're not a family. You work here. I live and work here." I suck on my peppermint.

"I want to go to the office and write."

"I want an apology," Ralph whines.

Paula pushes me to the office, sets up the computer, and leaves.

I open my inbox. I steady my breathing as I click the email from my publisher with the subject line: "Manuscript is accepted." I savor each sentence: *The manuscript, It's Another Life, is beautifully written showing a man's life with severe Cerebral palsy not many see. Our mission is to give readers an insight into unique lives. Your manuscript fits the description.* And the best sentence of all: *I want to offer you a contract. Rise Publishers, New York, New York.*

I yell, "I did it. New York, New York. I'm a New York author.

"I win, I win."

"Be quiet, I'm sleeping," Jimmy yells back from a different room.

"Fuck you. All you do is sleep. I had it. I did it. I win. I'm a New York author.

"Fuck you."

"Fuck you, Steve. I'm calling Jerry!" Jimmy shouts back.

We trade F-bombs back and forth.

Paula's footsteps pound on the floor. "What's going on?"

"Jimmy and Steve are arguing. Steve is very naughty. Tell him to stop it."

Ralph's voice is muffled in the hall.

"Go to hell, dummy."

I write my reply to Sarah Wilder, my publisher in New York.

"What's going on?" Paula barges into my office.

"I'm published again. A New York publisher wants to publish my third book. I'm a New York author."

"Congratulations." Paula wipes away my tears with a Kleenex. She prompts me to apologize with a side glare.

"Jimmy, I'm sorry for yelling," I call to him across the hallway.

"I just want quiet to sleep." Jimmy lets out a loud yawn.

"I'm sorry!" I yell to Jimmy, but he begins to snore.

"Go out! Celebrate your success. When was the last time you went out?" Paula asks.

"A month ago. I'm staying home to start another novel. I refuse to pay outrageous bus fare."

"You have to stop taking it out on Ralph." Paula leaves my room.

I start to tap my reply to the publisher when Kerry enters the office and closes the door.

She leans against my desk, arms crossed. "You have twenty-four hours to apologize to Ralph. If you don't: no computer, TV, or going out until you do. You know better."

She's right but I'm not a child. I decline to apologize. I stare at the corner. A cobweb sways ever so slightly.

"You will." Kerry powers down my computer.

"Go to hell."

"Twenty-four hours." Kerry leaves me to stew.

Confined to my office, staring at a blank screen, exaggerates my isolation. I need my computer. I don't enjoy talking to Ralph. For an hour, I go back and forth. Apologize. Don't. I choke down my resistance. I call to Teresa, "Have Ralph comes to my office." Ralph as usual is all forgiving.

The next day Jerry walks into the office. "Congratulations on the new book."

"I started a new novel last night."

"I hear you're making trouble with your roommates. And that you don't leave the house. Why?"

"Bus fare. It's not worth it. If I go, I want to spend an entire day downtown. Can my attendants meet me there to assist me to pee and eat on a Saturday or Sunday? I love it down there. I want to move downtown?" I ask Jerry. To travel back and forth from home to downtown for toileting and dining is ridiculous. I imagine living in an apartment and the freedom to cruise down State Street whenever I want.

"We have been through this. Your income isn't enough to afford an apartment and pay for care. My hands are tied, but I might be able to have attendants meet you downtown to assist you." Jerry looks at me. "Tonight, go somewhere.

Celebrate. Here's eight dollars. Where are you going?"

"Sal's." Staying home depresses me. By boycotting the bus, I have only hurt myself.

"I'll call the bus myself." Jerry dials the number. As he waits for them to answer, he asks me, "What time do you want to go?"

"Six-thirty to ten-thirty." A night out lifts my spirits.

When Jerry finishes the call, he turns to me and says, "Please go out sometimes. And be nice to Ralph. He's just a pup. Have you been getting laid?"

I avoid eye contact with him. "It takes five minutes and it's over." Sixty dollars is a lot of money for five minutes.

Sleet falls and the wind whips as I wait for the bus. Five minutes and my hands feel frostbitten. The wind howls, taking my breath away and loosens the head array. I retreat to the garage, but when I reach the garage the bus arrives.

Once inside of the bus, the warmth makes my normally tight muscles relax. I enjoy the ride. The lights glow in the dark since it is day light saving time. I taste freedom, riding down State Street to Sal's.

The bus driver, Neil, opens the door. "Go have fun—like drink or get laid."

I laugh thinking about Heather. At the bar, Doug drinks gin and tonic next to me. Wisconsin plays Michigan State in the Big Ten Basketball Championship Game. Sport enthusiasts cheer wildly when the Badgers score.

"What's up? We haven't seen you lately. We like you around. Want a beer?" He yells over the sound of the crowd.

"Miller."

Doug signals to Vin. The bartender nods.

"Is there a straw in the bag?" Doug searches for a straw in my backpack and pours the beer in a plastic cup. He gives me a sip. "Tell me when you want more."

"What's happening?" Fuzzy sits down at the bar on the other side of my electric wheelchair.

"Go Bucky." I scream the nickname of Wisconsin's Badger mascot.

"Welcome back, buddy!" Jesse pats me on the shoulder.

I nod, enjoying the nip and tuck game. Wisconsin trails by five points at halftime. I drink at time-outs, savoring being out among my new friends. This is worth a four-dollar bus ride.

"Do you want more beer?" Doug holds the empty cup at the ten-minute mark at the second half.

"No." My head array slips out of place.

The game is tight all the way to the final twenty seconds when the Badgers take a two-point lead, holding off the Spartans at the buzzer.

In the reverie, a college boy sloshes a beer on my shirt and arm. I smell like a brewery.

In celebration of the win, I accidently hit the readout with my left hand, bending it down making the readout difficult to see. The head array is cockeyed.

The victory feels great, but I know that I have a problem with driving the wheelchair.

I feel like one of the guys.

"See you for the tournament. You're good luck. Until the next time," The guys say, making me part of their group.

Guiding the electric wheelchair is a chore. It doesn't steer straight, but I manage to negotiate the wheelchair out of the door and to the bus. It takes me five minutes to mount the ramp. I'm tired. The wheelchair is crooked and I can't see the readout.

The bus driver says, "Put the seat down and straighten out the wheelchair. I won't load you if you don't."

"I can't drive. It's bent."

"I can't help you. You reek of alcohol. You shouldn't go to places like this alone. You need an attendant with you at all times." Mark holds the lift control box in his hand, waiting to operate the automatic ramp.

That sets me off. Jerry doesn't allow care attendants in bars.

"Fuck you."

"I'm reporting this to Metro Mobility." Mark goes inside the bus and radios the dispatcher.

I say the F word several times. I'm upset. It frustrates me that the wheelchair isn't working and I'm losing my independence. I am wrong for yelling at Mark, and now they may take away my bus riding privileges. I have already cut back on my bus rides.

I try to tilt the electric wheelchair seat down. I can't see the seating mechanism readout. My muscles spaz as I panic.

A pretty woman comes out of nowhere. "Can I help you?"

I point to the monitor, using my left hand.

"Do you mean this?" The woman pulls the box up, allowing me to see the seating device readout. This gives me the ability to lower the seat, maneuver the electric wheelchair, and board the ramp. I wait for Mark to return and raise the lift.

"Thank you." I smile at her.

"You're quite welcome." The woman seems pleased that she'd solved my problem.

Mark returns. "You shouldn't be out here. I'm writing you up tomorrow.

"You mean that he shouldn't be out by himself at the bar," The woman chides him.

Mark nods. His answer angers me.

"Fuck you." I embarrass myself in front of the woman. My temper gives the impression I'm cognitively disabled and drunk.

"Let's get you on the bus." Mark raises the ramp.

"Don't write me up. I need to go out. I'm sorry but I don't have much freedom anymore. Please, Mark."

"We all have jobs. I work hard, too. I don't have to put up with your shit. It doesn't make sense for you to be out here alone getting drunk in bars. You need an attendant with you. And that's that." Mark buckles his seat belt. "I'm done talking with you."

"I guess I'll kill myself."

No response from Mark.

My body crumples in frustration. The street lights pass on the road to Clove house. I ask myself why I create barriers that threaten my independence. I want to see people and grab onto life, curious of the journey I may take.

One of my new care attendants, June, greets us in front of the garage.

Mark disengages the electric wheelchair and pushes it onto the ramp. June pushes me inside. "Oh, creepers, I can fix that." June inspects the bent head array and retrieves an Allen wrench. Five minutes later, the head array is as good as new.

"It must have been a great game. Your shirt stinks of beer."

The phone rings and June answers it. "He's here and he isn't drunk. I can't smell any alcohol on his breath." Pause. "His head array needed adjusting. I did it and it works just fine now." Pause. "The bus driver wouldn't change from manual mode. I had enough. I pushed

Steve inside." Pause. "Sure, I'll put him on speaker. Just a minute."

"You did nothing wrong," Kerry's voice says through the speaker. "Are you okay?"

I tell her that I'm okay, even though I'm not.

People make judgments about me. I feel angry and hurt by Mark. In the past, the electric wheelchair has broken down with minor repairs often when Mark was driving. It isn't his job to deal with my broken wheelchair. I can see how he believed that I was drunk and I needed an attendant with me.

I consider staying in fearing my privilege of using the bus will be taken away.

After spending over one hundred dollars of my own money to purchase thirty-six bus tickets, I conserve my rides.

"Are you going out this week or Saturday?" Kerry folds my laundry. Fabric softener freshness springs in the air.

"No."

She wants to cut double coverage for Clove house in order for Integration to save money. No second attendant to assist means I won't have a shower on the weekend or transfers to the electric wheelchair for a stroll in the neighborhood. One attendant must remain on premises when Jimmy's in the house.

"You don't go out much. Why?"

"It's a hassle. I feel sorry for people who take the bus every day. How do you tell someone like Ralph that he can't afford to take the bus to go to work? It's a contradiction."

"It's a mess." Kerry untangles a bed sheet.

"Can an attendant meet me downtown on the weekend to assist me with the urinal and eat? That way I can stay downtown an entire day without taking a second round-trip, saving me money." I asked before but didn't get an answer.

"We can't afford that and we can't go with you."

I treasure being on my own and out among people. I like my attendants, but going places alone offers an escape from the small problems with the staff. It is like I'm a rebellious teenager, who believes he doesn't need his parents, but still needs help with money or doing the laundry.

I don't want an attendant with me when I go to The Silver Spoon or Sal's. The time away from my staff is golden. I savor my independence, but I still need some assistance when I'm out in the community for an entire day. I'm lucky I can forgo eating and can go several hours without having to urinate, but eventually nature calls.

Several beers fill a bladder quickly. Often, I pee in my pants out in public or at establishments. It embarrasses me but I don't know what else to do. I think about wearing a catheter, but catheters hurt and need to be emptied. Asking strangers or acquaintances for assistance to use the bathroom is out of the question. I often want to ask Doug, Fuzzy or Fire to help me to use the restroom, but that's asking too much of them.

My dream of having a girlfriend makes me imagine having a woman to take me to the bathroom. I picture having Fire holding the urinal. Not so romantic. I have trouble going at first, but she encourages me. "I have seen guys' dicks before and yours is like any other. Now just go."

I have stopped going places after the incident with Mark. I hide in my office, writing another book or doing publicity for my new novel. When I'm in my bedroom, I try to sleep to escape the pain of loneliness, but I watch sports or porn instead. I masturbate sometimes but sex isn't always on my mind. It pops into my head now and then, but I want a relationship.

I work on selling myself to the news media, but I'm old news to the local news. My creative juices stall on ideas to refresh my image.

That's an author's life. It goes up and down during a single day. I sigh, hating publicity, but it is a part of the career. Feeling defeated, I lick my wounds.

My computer dings with a new email from Kate, the occupational therapist from Point College. The installation of your new computer and the communication device is Friday.

I'm tempted to tell Kate to forget it. In fact, I write a reply, saying that I don't want it anymore. But I don't send it. It is stupid after spending four thousand dollars from my trust fund and that doesn't include the eighteen hundred dollars for Kate's services. I can't give up.

The only place I go to now is Sal's to watch the

Packers with the guys and drink. Nothing like the Packers winning in the last seconds of a game or in overtime.

I ask Paula to transfer me to the electric wheelchair to work on the communication device. I haven't done anything with it for two months since Kate visited.

Paula stops me. "After my lunch break."

I watch CNN. The new computer is up, but the staff doesn't give me the extra help to get the computer working. I have to wait fifteen minutes for a glass of water. Their phone calls are more important than caring for me. Sometimes going to Walgreens or Integration's office takes precedence over giving me a shower.

Integration has cut more attendant hours, upsetting their employees and providing inadequate care. It seems Integration is more concerned about overtime than the clients' well-being, but Jerry's hands are tied due to cuts in Medicaid. I want to blame Jerry, but he loves all of his clients, including the author, who emails him at two in the morning with another complaint.

No computer means no complaints from me. I want to make Clove House a living hell. I fall asleep watching Wolf Blizter.

Brian, my counselor, knocks on my door, waking me up. "Can I come in?"

I shake off the sleep.

"How's the new computer? Is it working?" Brian sits down in my recliner.

I'm wide awake and passionate about the topic. "I can make it work, but I need help from my attendants.

They're too busy," I say in a loud voice so they overhear our conversation.

"I'm going to explode. The staff doesn't help me so you're going to be over here every day if I can't write. I'm an author. I don't want excuses. I don't give a shit about their stupid paperwork. And lunch breaks or errands take an hour. I'm a New York author."

"I know." Brian pats me on the shoulder. "I'll talk to Jerry after we get done and we'll get you writing soon. I promise."

"My computer is my life and I don't go out. I haven't been any place for two months."

"Why?"

"The bus, I can't afford the fare increase. I slowly quit going places. That's what people don't understand. I miss people, especially women." I start to cry. "I need to go somewhere."

"Then go. Where do you want to go?"

I think for a moment before answering, "Sal's 6:30 to 10:30."

"I'll have Paula set it up now."

I sit at the bar, watching the Milwaukee Bucks versus the Indiana Pacers and the Milwaukee Brewers versus the Chicago Cubs. Two TVs are necessary during early spring for the NBA playoffs and the start of the baseball season. After I find a place at the bar, I recline the electric wheelchair back a bit to relax. I look for Doug, Fuzzy, and Allen, but they are not here tonight.

"Good to see you." Vin, the bartender smiles at me,

walking back and forth behind the bar. Now and then Vin gives me a sip of beer.

I'm out of Clove house away from my computer and staff. I sit back enjoying the atmosphere, music playing, all the people. I savor the night and I decide to spend eighty dollars a month on the bus for nights out.

I don't want to sit at home, writing while life goes on without me. I will have to be frugal about where I go and stay home sometimes even when I don't want to. Being in the bar gives me a new perspective on the larger picture.

A pretty woman comes over to me. "Hi, I'm Jackie. What's your name?"

"Steve. I'm an author. I have two books out this year. What do you do?"

"I don't work. Two years ago, my mother passed away. It is so hard." Jackie sips her beer.

It's eerie, hearing her talk about the death of her Mom. "I know. My Mom died two years ago, too. I do it all by myself now. I do my best. It hurts being alone. I'm tired of being alone and want a girlfriend."

"You're a handsome man with a career." Jackie squeezes my hand. "My boyfriend has a learning disability and works in a warehouse. We live together and plan to get married."

I'm crestfallen hoping she is the one. "Will I ever have a girlfriend?"

"Someday you will." Jackie gives me a hug.

I watch her walk away. "Yes, someday."

ACKNOWLEDGEMENTS

I want to thank Integrity Residential Services especially my staff, Rachel Kaiser, and Steve Lawrence. It is not easy caring for an author. I want to thank my cat, Lindy, who is always there for me. A special thanks goes to Rita Angelini, Tim Storm, and Kristine Hansen, who offered writing advice. I have to thank my family: Susan Bain, Jennifer Tonn, Trent Tonn, Jon Bain, John DiVall, and Sara DiVall. My college classmates have always been a source of inspiration to me. Thank you, Amber Tilley, Dave Strong, Christine Evans, and Jessie Bushman. I'm indebted to the Writer's Institute especially Laurie Scheer and Christine DeSmet. An author needs creative people to support them in good and bad times. The authors have been there for me when I needed a pep talk: Larry Watson, Lisa Kaiser, Valerie Beil, Bob Curry, and Andy Millman. I want to thank the following people Suzan Kurry, Stasia Wilson, Michael Lussenden, Patti Huber, William Patrick Barlow, William Colby, Tanaya Crawford, Que Campbell, Sam Smith, Jenny Adams, Beth Engelhart, Tim

Hinze, Cleone Reed, Tina Schwartz, Jennifer Mastick, and Doug Moe. A thank you goes to Whiskey Jacks, my bar, and Visions Night Club.

About the Author

Steven uses Morse code to write since he is unable to use his hands, swaying his head back and forth tapping one letter at a time. Every five seconds a character pops up on the computer screen. He earned a Bachelor of Science in English with a writing minor from the University of Wisconsin-Stevens Point. Also, Steven has a Liberal Arts degree from Madison College. He writes a newsletter for Integrity Residential Services. Currently, Steven is writing his tenth manuscript. His book *It's A New Life! Mom Is Gone* is available on Amazon. Steven enjoys watching the Packers, basketball with friends and the outdoors. He lives in Madison, Wisconsin with his cat, Lindy.

To learn more about Steven, please visit
www.stevenbsalmon.com.

If you enjoyed this book, please leave a review on your favorite website.

~ Thank you